LANCA**S**

MEDI**H**

MONAS**T**

LANCASHIRE'S
MEDIEVAL MONASTERIES

Brian Marshall
(B.A., M.Phil.)

Landy Publishing
2006

The author, Brian Marshall, claims copyright in the text of this book. The terms of the Copyright, Designs and Patents Act 1988 and the Duration of Copyright & Rights in Performance Regulations 1995 are to be applied.

ISBN. 1 872895 68 9

A catalogue record of this book is available from the British Library

Layout by Sue Clarke

Printed by
Nayler Group, Aero Mill, Church, Accrington
Tel 01254 234247

Landy Publishing have also published:

Traipsing from a Lancashire Toll Bar: Bretherton, Croston, Hesketh Bank, Hoole, Tarleton & Walmer Bridge in Focus by Betty Gilkes & Stan Pickles
Glimpses of Glasson Dock & Vicinity by Ruth Z Roskell
Life on the Lancaster Canal by Janet Rigby
Play Up, Higher Walton by Peter Holme
Northward by Anthony Hewitson
Preston in Focus by Stephen Sartin
Cockersand Abbey, Lancashire by Brian Marshall
Penwortham, Hutton & Longton in Focus by Catherine Rees
Bolland Forest & the Hodder Valley by Greenwood & Bolton
A History of Pilling by Frank Sobee

A full list is available from

Landy Publishing,
"Acorns", 3 Staining Rise, Staining, Blackpool. FY3 0BU
Tel & Fax 01253 895678

CONTENTS

FOREWORD

It gives me great pleasure to introduce this fine book to what I know will be a large and highly appreciative reading public. The author, Brian Marshall, is a deeply learned scholar who has worked for a considerable number of years on the history of the Lancashire monasteries and their landholdings. Yet, as an experienced teacher, Brian is able to convey his scholarship in an absolutely clear and reader-friendly way. His prose is indeed always readable and enjoyable, and often beautiful - especially when he conveys to us his intimate knowledge of his beloved Lancashire countryside. This wide-ranging study makes an immense contribution to county history. Brian has chosen a list of monasteries from around the historic county and he reveals the vital role those religious houses played in the social and economic, but above all in the spiritual and religious, life of medieval Lancastrians. This is a book to read by a winter fireside or to put on the top of the picnic basket, to accompany a summer circuit tour of the lovely and sad ruins and remnants, the bared ruin'd choirs where once the sweet birds sang.

Michael Mullett
Professor of Cultural and Religious History
University of Lancaster

INTRODUCTION

Monasticism in medieval Europe was a spiritual, social and economic phenomenon the like of which had never been seen before and has certainly not been repeated. There had been monasteries and monks since the earlier years of the Church but never in such numbers as were to appear from the tenth century to the sixteenth, when a profound level of spirituality inspired tens of thousands to renounce the world and assume the garb of the monk, seeking primarily the salvation of their souls through a life of communal prayer and spiritual devotion. For a variety of reasons, the monastic life was not open to most people and so the monks extended the scope of their prayers and intercessions to embrace the spiritual needs of others. Chief among the beneficiaries of monastic prayer were the founders of the countless abbeys, priories and friaries that proliferated from Sweden to Spain and from Bohemia to the British Isles. England alone had around 1,000 religious houses of one kind or another and it would be impossible to enumerate the total founded across Europe. These religious houses represented the spiritual focus of millions of people who saw them as a safeguard against the onset of evil and a major aid in the salvation of their souls; they provided extensive services such as schools, hospitals, midwifery, poor relief and retirement homes, none of which would have been available to ordinary folk without the charity of the monks; and as major landowners they played a large part in the rural economy as well as providing employment for huge numbers of people.

Christian monasticism is an institution almost as old as the Church itself. As early as the third century we find groups of holy men setting up a communal existence in the deserts of Egypt, Palestine and Syria, far from the distractions of normal life, so as to create a deeply spiritual environment in which to bring themselves closer to God. Chief among these, perhaps, was Saint Anthony of Egypt, 251-356, who spent almost the whole of his long life as an ascetic in the desert. This monastic practice found

5

its way into Europe through Constantinople and Rome, and under the auspices of the later Roman Empire such major figures as Augustine of Hippo (now the city of Bone in Algeria), 354-450, and Benedict of Nursia, (modern Norcia situated north east of Rome) d. c.550, set out codes for the conduct of monastic establishments: documents that were to become the foundation for the great monastic orders of the middle ages. Indeed, the Rule of St. Benedict and the Rule of St. Augustine still govern the lives of the contemplative orders in the twenty-first century. Neither Benedict nor Augustine, however, can have envisaged the extent of the following that his particular prescription for the religious life was to engender in the centuries that lay ahead.

At the end of the sixth century, when another Augustine was sent by Pope Gregory the Great, (590-604) to evangelise the pagan English he brought with him a number of priests who were monks following the Rule of Benedict, as indeed he was himself. A few monasteries were established in England in the centuries between Augustine's arrival and the Norman Conquest but, although many of the clergy were monks, there was no great upsurge of monasticism and when England fell to the Normans in 1066 there were fewer than fifty religious houses and barely a thousand monks and nuns in the whole country.

A hundred and fifty years before the Normans came to England, however, continental Europe had witnessed the beginning of a truly remarkable display of religious devotion that saw large numbers of men, and considerably fewer women, giving over their lives to a daily round of prayer. They sought the salvation of their immortal souls through prayer and self-denial, and of the souls of others by interceding with God on behalf of their benefactors in particular, and of humanity at large. This fervour first appeared at the beginning of the tenth century, rose to a peak around the thirteenth and began to change direction in the fifteenth, when new forms of religious thought started to lead Europe towards the Reformation.

England, at the time of the Conquest, was somewhat out of touch with the development of religious thought and practice on the Continent. Though solidly Christian, the English tended not to display the fervour and depth of spirituality that characterised much of Western Europe in the tenth and eleventh centuries. This spirituality first manifested itself at Cluny in Burgundy where a new monastic ideal grew in the great monastery founded there in 910 by William, Count of Auvergne and Duke of Aquitaine. The monks of Cluny adhered to the Rule of St. Benedict but were determined that monasteries should be free from involvement in the feudal system that was now shaping the social, economic and political life of western Europe, and of which the Benedictine houses had become a part. Though most of the religious houses in Europe subscribed to the Benedictine rule, each individual house followed its own path. There was no Benedictine 'Order,' such as came into being later in the middle ages. Cluny, however, brought discipline and a common observance of the rule of St. Benedict, not just within the abbey itself but in all its many daughter houses that sprang up throughout Europe. Now for the first time we had a monastic order. Though they still professed adherence to the Rule of St. Benedict the Cluniacs were clearly a separate group. All Cluniac houses were to be priories, that is, houses of subordinate status, except the mother house itself which was the order's only abbey, and all priors, in whatever country their houses might be situate were subordinate and answerable to the Abbot of Cluny.

The phenomenon of Cluny set the tone for the growth of spirituality and the contemplative life throughout Europe, and within a century or so there appeared another monastic body: groups of clergy living the communal, spiritual life and following the Rule of Saint Augustine. These came to be known as the Augustinian, or Austin, canons, their houses more numerous than those of any other order. Because they lived according to a Rule, (Latin *Regulus*), they were also referred to as the Canons Regular. While the Benedictines maintained their time-honoured practices, the Cluniacs were confident in the regimen they now followed, and the canons regular were busy providing temporal as well as spiritual services for the lay communities among whom they tended to live, still the quest for a deeper spirituality and a higher level of Christian devotion continued.

An event occurred in 1098 that was of greater magnitude even than the birth of the Cluniac movement. In that year a number of dissident Benedictine monks at Molesme in Burgundy quit their abbey and set up a new establishment at Cîteaux, sometimes known by its Latin name, *Cistercium*. These monks, led by their abbot, Robert, declared that they remained Benedictine though they were not happy at the laxity that had crept into the observance of the Rule, and so, in their new home, they intended to apply the spirit as well as the letter of what Benedict had intended some six centuries earlier. Two developments occurred rapidly, the first of which was the setting up of daughter houses, the second, the recognition of these breakaway Benedictines as a new order, known as the Cistercians after the site of their original house. Within a relatively short time the Cistercian houses were numbered in hundreds, many of them very large.

Other new orders came into being over the next century or so, though none was to have the same impact on European society, either spiritually or materially, as that made by the Cistercians. The most notable of these later groups was the Premonstratensian order of canons regular. They followed the

Augustinian rule but, like the Cistercians with the Benedictine rule, they observed it more rigorously.

By the end of the twelfth century there had been a proliferation of monasteries throughout Europe, with many thousands of men and women committing themselves to the contemplative life bound by vows of poverty, chastity and obedience. Their purpose was to save their own souls and the souls of others by perpetual acts of prayer and devotion, while they also, and the Augustinian canons in particular, cared for the poor and needy, while closely engaged in teaching and preaching.

These holy men and women, who imposed upon themselves such austere conditions in the name of God, were the leaders of Christian thought and practice. They represented the aspirations of a society that believed earnestly in the salvation, or damnation, of the soul and perceived itself as being under constant attack by the powers of evil led by Satan. The Christian people of Europe were glad to have among them these stalwart warriors of Christ who lived in dwellings like military barracks and waged constant war against the dark powers on their behalf.

The Creation of a Monastery

A medieval monastery was not an establishment founded by monks. Its founder was almost invariably a lay magnate who called the house into being for the purpose of having the monks or canons devote their lives of prayer and religious devotion to interceding with God for the souls of himself and his family: on the whole the richer the founder, the larger the house. The people of medieval Europe believed in the power of intercession - that Almighty God might be influenced by prayer offered on behalf of

9

one person by another. Also of critical importance was the doctrine of purgatory which held that a soul might be deemed unfit for heaven yet be not bad enough to be condemned to hell. For these there was purgatory, a state somewhere between heaven and hell in which souls might languish until redeemed by the prayers of the faithful on earth. Who better to offer such prayers than holy monks, men whose very profession it was to intercede with God on behalf of others?

With the arrival of the Normans there came a surge of monastery building in England. Norman barons and knights had been accustomed to setting up monasteries in their homeland and they quickly made use of their newly acquired estates in England for the same purpose. William the Conqueror himself began the process by founding the great Benedictine abbeys of Battle, on the site of the Battle of Hastings, and Selby on crown estate in East Yorkshire. Suitable land would be set aside by the founder for the building of his new monastery and further estates added for the upkeep of the buildings and the livelihood of the monks. In return for his munificence, he asked nothing more than the prayers of the monks in perpetuity, so that during his lifetime, and far beyond, while his soul might be confined to purgatory, a community of holy men would be praying for him, his family and heirs, and in some cases, the king. In fact, medieval society was made up of three estates: those who worked, those who fought, and those who prayed; the last group specialising in praying for the other two.

Other landowners, large and small, would make use of this newly built 'manufactory of prayer' by making to it donations, so that they too might benefit from prayers said on their behalf by the monks. It was indeed common for great or popular religious houses to receive gifts of whole estates: often manors of 4,000 or

5,000 acres, in return for nothing more than the prayers of the monks. Lesser landowners might donate 1,000 acres, a 100 acres, five acres, half an acre, all for the purpose of obtaining the perpetual prayers of the monks or canons. Thus, some houses became wealthy indeed, with estates of 50,000 or 60,000 acres and more, and incomes that placed them on a level with the richest barons in the land.

It was not only land that was given to the monasteries in this way. Many kinds of money-making or money-saving benefaction were bestowed upon them by those keen to make every possible provision for the salvation of their souls. Most valuable of these assets were churches. Before the Reformation, churches belonged to individuals, usually the lord of the manor or some other wealthy individual, rather than to the parish or diocese. They were therefore his property to do with as he saw fit. All the income in terms of fees for services, collections, oblations, tithes and the like came to him. The priest was normally appointed by the owner and paid a stipend. Large numbers of churches were given to monasteries, some having as many as twenty-five, and their income representing a major part of the annual turnover of the religious houses. Also given to monasteries were water rights, fisheries, rights of pasture, rights to timber, rights of way, water mills, fulling mills and many more assets that would be of financial benefit.

Despite strictures and prohibitions enjoined by the new monastic orders, particularly the Cluniacs and Cistercians, against ownership of extensive property, receiving of tithes, ownership of churches and general participation in the manorial/feudal order, they were inexorably drawn into it. By the thirteenth century we find not only abbots of the great Benedictine houses such as Ramsey, Glastonbury and Westminster, but also Cistercian abbots of such houses as Rievaulx, Fountains and Furness, and the priors of large Cluniac houses: Lewes, Bermondsey and Montacute for example, ranked with the most powerful men in the land. Even

11

small priories, with little more than a couple of thousand acres held lordships of the manor in their own right, their priors exercising the rights and duties of that office. This wealth and status was not sought by the monks; generally they did not solicit gifts from the rich and powerful. Rather it was the benefactors themselves who heaped this largesse upon the monastic communities in the quest for eternal life. However, by about the end of the thirteenth century the practice of land donation to monasteries in England had more or less come to an end. A number of laws of *mortmain*, made by Edward I, 1270-1307, regarding the consequences of such transactions rendered the receiving of land in this way an unattractive proposition for religious houses.

Yet from the late eleventh century to the early fourteenth the monasteries of England had come, collectively, into possession of vast areas of land; perhaps as much as a third of the total agricultural land in the country. Not all monasteries were large of course, and many were far from rich, but all depended, not only on the area of land they held, but also on its quality. A house that held boggy, ill-drained land could hardly prosper on it, and such was the case with a number of the houses founded in Lancashire.

Early Lancashire

The area we know as Lancashire was, at the time of the Norman Conquest, a poor and underdeveloped region, with a population of perhaps little more than 10,000 people and no significant town other than Preston. Much of it was either peat bog or moor and was little sought after by the victorious Norman knights and barons.

As late as the seventeenth century the writer Gervase Markham (1570-1655) declared that:

Lancashire is one of the most barren counties in England, a country more backward agriculturally than most countries of Europe.

There was not even a county of Lancashire until the late twelfth century, when it was one of the last of the modern shires to come into existence. In the great surge of monastery building that England experienced after the Conquest, Lancashire saw nothing like the scale of monastic settlement that occurred in, for example, Yorkshire, Lincolnshire or Norfolk. Nonetheless, thirteen monastic houses were built, three of them of considerable size. Five orders of monks or canons were represented: the Benedictines had four houses: Lancaster, Penwortham, Lytham and Upholland; the Augustinians four: Conishead, Cartmel, Burscough and Cockerham; the Cistercians two: Furness and Whalley; the Premonstratensians two: Hornby and Cockersand; and the Cluniacs one, namely the cell at Kersal. There were also four friaries representing the Dominicans at Lancaster, the Franciscans at both Preston and Lancaster and the Augustinian Friars at Warrington.

Largest and richest of all the Lancashire houses was the Cistercian Furness Abbey which held extensive agricultural and pastoral estates and carried on a considerable trade in iron-smelting, quarrying and merchant shipping. There are major ruins at Furness that include some fine Romanesque arches, an elaborate sedilia and significant parts of the church, more than 300 feet in length. Like other monasteries of north Lancashire, Furness suffered serious despoliation at the hands of Scottish raiders.

13

Monasteries were dependent for their survival largely on the estates they possessed and the efficiency with which these were handled by their abbots or priors. Some of the houses set up granges from which to control their distant estates. Furness, Whalley and Cockersand all had lay-brothers living in these granges as stewards of lands too far away to be run from the abbeys themselves. Unfortunately, much of the land held by Lancashire monasteries was of poor quality and from time to time the monks found themselves having to bring in food from elsewhere. By the middle of the fourteenth century monasteries, in common with non-monastic landowners, were no longer relying on their lands for food and on the sale of their produce for an income. There was a large-scale shift to the practice of renting, and abbots, like the barons and the gentry, became country landowners making their income by letting their estates to tenants.

We have a great deal of contemporaneous documentation on which to draw and we can learn much of the lifestyle of these medieval figures. There are the reports of visitations or inspections by bishops, sometimes telling us that all was as it should be, but occasionally recording wrongdoings that include: minor breaches of dress, dissatisfaction with the food, carrying of knives, wounding, murder and witchcraft. We also hear of sodomy and illicit sexual liaisons with women.

A number of the smaller Lancashire monasteries were not independent in their own right but were cells of major houses. Lytham Priory belonged to Durham Cathedral Priory, Penwortham Priory to Evesham Abbey, Hornby Priory to Croxton Abbey, Lancaster Priory to St. Martin's Abbey in Normandy, Cockerham Priory to Leicester Abbey, and Kersal Priory to Lenton Abbey. From time to time these arrangements caused disputes, and occasionally violence, between the monks resident in the satellite house and their superiors in the mother-house, often over the question of rendering dues but sometimes over the issue of independence.

Some interesting characters are clearly seen across the centuries. Several Cockersand canons are named as transgressors of the vow of chastity, along with the women with whom they were involved. One of these men, James Skipton, was found guilty of serious sexual lapses and banished to a distant abbey for seven years, but came back and was eventually appointed abbot of Cockersand. Most notorious was Roger Norris, prior of Penwortham, who fornicated, cheated, lied, embezzled and brought the house to virtual bankruptcy but, because the abbot of Evesham was not answerable to a mother-house, he chose to keep Norris in office at Penwortham rather than bring him back to Evesham. Other un-monastic activities included the fraternal relationship that existed between the Augustinian Canons of Cartmel Priory and the Augustinian canons of Dublin Cathedral. The two groups exchanged frequent convivial visits that had little to do with their religious duties.

From the founding of the first Lancashire monastery in 1094 to the suppression in 1539 of Cockersand Abbey, the last of them to close, the religious houses, poor though most of them were, played their part in the religious life of the county and also in the economic development of significant parts of it. Attitudes and perceptions changed, however, over 400 years, and by the sixteenth century there were those who placed little value on the

15

monks' powers of intercession on their behalf, and some who had begun to covet the estates held by institutions they saw increasingly as irrelevant. It was the king, however, who brought about the closure of the monasteries. Henry VIII, like most monarchs, was always in need of ready money and his advisers were quick to tell him how it could be obtained. There were more than 700 abbeys and priories in England, together with some 300 friaries, hospitals and colleges, all of which held estates large or small and whose assets, if confiscated by the crown, would be of enormous benefit to the royal exchequer.

The End of the Monasteries

Between 1536 and 1540 the process of dissolution was completed, quietly and compliantly by some houses, but resisted by others. In the north of England large numbers of people saw royal seizure of the monastic houses and their assets as intolerable and there was organised resistance that amounted to insurrection and came to be known as the Pilgrimage of Grace, 1536-7. Though there were various causes of this rising against royal authority most of the participants saw it as a religious cause and declared that they were engaged in a pilgrimage.

The Dissolution of the Monasteries was doubly tragic for the Lancashire houses, involved as some of them were in the revolt. At least two came to an end in bloodshed, and all suffered partial, and in some cases, total, destruction of their buildings. At

Whalley the abbot and two of his monks were hanged, while at Cartmel, the house having already been closed, some of the canons returned during the Pilgrimage of Grace and several of these were hanged for treason, along with ten local men. On the other hand, a number of houses passed quietly out of existence. At Cockersand the abbot accepted a pension of £40 per annum, around £13,400 in 2006, and his canons £6, a little over £2,000, leaving the abbey and vanishing from our sight.

Some of the sites are still clearly to be identified with their past. There are major remains at Furness and Whalley. At Cockersand there is little but the thirteenth- century chapter house, which is the best example of its kind in England, but the site retains an aura of sanctity. At Burscough there are two elegant piers only, but these suggest a very handsome church. A number of the monastery churches survive in use as parish churches. The splendid fifteenth-century church at Lancaster is much admired and visited, as is the superb church of Cartmel. The church of Cockerham Priory is still present though much modernised, and at Upholland Priory the nave of the present church was once the chancel of the priory church.

Despite the poverty of the land and the paucity of monastic foundation within it, the history of Lancashire monasticism is as rich, varied and interesting as that of any shire in England. It provides a clear vision of all that monasticism meant to ordinary folk and demonstrates how, regardless of the small number of religious houses, the influence of monks was an important part of the lives of just about everyone in the county.

The line drawings within the text are taken from a book on styles of architecture in England by Thomas Rickman (1848). They are in either the 'Norman' (c. 1059 -1200) or 'Early English' style (c. 1200 – 1300).

LANCASTER PRIORY

The small Benedictine monastery founded at Lancaster in 1094 was an *'Alien Priory,'* one of some 160 in England so designated. After the Conquest of 1066, many of the Norman barons and knights founded monasteries on their newly acquired estates. A considerable number of these victorious Normans were already founders and patrons of monasteries in their homeland and took this opportunity to bestow further wealth upon these houses founded by, and connected with, their families. Such a family was the de Montgomery family to which belonged Roger of Poitou, one of the principal Norman commanders and holder of major estates in North-West England. His family had founded, at Séez in Normandy, the abbey of Saint Martin, and Roger diverted to it a significant portion of the assets of his English holdings.

In 1094, as part of his benefactions to Saint Martin's, Roger gave the church of Lancaster together with various estates and tithes. The abbot of Séez sent a small group of his monks to Lancaster to run the parish and estate, and so the *'Alien Priory'* of Lancaster came into existence. Such houses throughout England were known as 'alien' because they were the property of a foreign monastery and usually, as at Lancaster, they did not recruit locally, their monks being exclusively provided by the mother-house on the continent. To a large French or Norman abbey a church, priory or estate held in England was simply a source of income, regarded in the same way as a monastery in Cheshire might regard an estate held in Lancashire.

The monastic community resident at Lancaster priory was small, consisting initially of a prior, five monks, three secular priests and two clerks. For the first hundred years or so of its existence it was not *'conventual,'* functioning more as a rectory than a monastery. The reason for this number of clergy was the serving of some of the churches belonging to the priory at one time or another. The prior was effectively rector of a large parish,

18

controlling part, or in some cases, all, of the resources of churches and chapels other than Lancaster, that had been donated to the monks. These included: Heysham, Melling, and Bolton-le-Sands, Preston, Kirkham, , Poulton-le-Fylde, Croston, a moiety of Eccleston and Childwall in Lancashire; Cotgrave and Crophill in Nottinghamshire and Wakerley, Northamptonshire. Soon added were the chapels of Gressingham and Caton in Lonsdale and Stalmine and Bispham in Amounderness. By 1246, Lancaster Priory retained an interest in only five churches, the rest having been transferred for one reason or another. Those with which it was still concerned were: Lancaster and Poulton, which were fully appropriated, Heysham, Croston and Eccleston, of which it continued to hold the advowson.

By the early thirteenth century most of the churches associated with Lancaster Priory were given away or exchanged. That of Melling, for example, was transferred to the Montbegon family of Hornby at a date between 1185 and 1210. The Montbegons in return resigned all claim to the chapel of Gressingham. It was about this time that the small community of Benedictine monks at Lancaster became 'conventual'; that is: they began to follow the daily round of offices usually associated with the monastic life. This required attendance at the monastery church some nine times in each twenty-four hour cycle and was referred to as 'keeping the hours.' They also assumed a corporate identity making decisions affecting the house in the name of the prior and monks of Lancaster.

An establishment of such limited proportions as Lancaster Priory did not have the resources of a Furness or a Fountains but nonetheless the provisions made for it by Roger and other benefactors gave the monks a very comfortable existence and produced significant profit for the mother-house in Normandy. In 1413 the net income of the priory was £110, the equivalent of something in excess of £42,000 in 2006. This, of course, being net, meant that it was the sum available to send to Saint Martin of Séez for one year, all debts and dues having been paid.

Roger's provision for his Lancaster monks was generous. He gave them the tithes of nineteen townships, together with those of the parishes of Preston and Bolton-le-Sands. They also received a tenth part of the pannage, hunting and fishing of all Roger's Lancashire estate. The Domesday survey of 1086-7 records that the northern part of Lancashire was an under-populated, unproductive area. There were 62 vills, or townships, in the hundred of Amounderness of which only sixteen had people living in them. The other 46 were said to be waste. The sixteen inhabited vills are not named but we might suppose that when Roger gave the tithes of certain vills to his newly arrived monks at Lancaster in the name of Saint Martin of Séez, he did not select those that were no more than waste. Such donations were an act of religious charity and a practical measure for the support of the monks, and what he had in mind represented commodities the monks could use for their subsistence.

The first townships required to render tithe to the Lancaster monks were: Preston, Ribby, Singleton and Preesall which were to give one tenth of: fowls, calves, lambs, goats, hogs, corn, cheese and butter. These are practical commodities for the use of a newly arrived group of men and we might reasonably accept that the four townships were among the sixteen said in Domesday, only eight years earlier, to be inhabited.

By comparison with many other monasteries, Lancaster Priory was not endowed with extensive lands. An important part of what was given to the monks by Roger was the land they held around Lancaster. It consisted chiefly of the town of Lancaster, together with the manors of Aldcliffe: 1,016 acres, and Bulk: 1,158 acres. This area would have been the 'home-farm,' producing much of the food required by the monks. The other township in which Lancaster Priory had a major holding was Poulton-le-Fylde. Approximately half of the land in Poulton, some 600 acres, had been given to Lancaster Priory; about 450 acres by Roger, the rest in relatively small parcels by a number of later donors. Poulton, with a wealthy church at its heart, and little moss (peat bog), was an important part of Lancaster's estate. In the twelfth and thirteenth centuries it was run as a manor to the considerable profit of the Priory. Probably by 1300, however, and certainly after the Black Death, which struck Lancashire in 1349-50, the agricultural land of Poulton, in common with most monastic estates in England, was being let by the prior to tenants.

 Monastic landowners, like landowners of every kind, found themselves in dispute from time to time with those who held land adjacent to their own, and Lancaster Priory seems to have been prone to litigation with its neighbours, often other monasteries. Because of the limited extent of the land held by the Lancaster monks they depended heavily on dues payable to them as temporalities and spiritualities, in particular the tithes of a considerable number of townships. The payment and collection of such dues was often highly contentious, as we see in the case of the priory's Poulton estate. Included in the parish of Poulton were the townships of Staining, Hardhorn and Newton, and although Lancaster did not hold the land there it was entitled, as owner of the parish church, to receive the tithe. The three vills were actually held by the Cistercian Stanlaw Abbey in Cheshire, which was abandoned in the late thirteenth century

and its monks transferred to Lancashire where they founded Whalley Abbey. The situation was that Stanlaw, later Whalley, was required to pay tithe on these lands to Lancaster Priory as holder of the parish of Poulton. The matter was simplified in 1234 when the two houses agreed that Stanlaw should collect the tithes for itself and pay Lancaster the sum of five marks in lieu. This did not settle the issue, however, as in 1260 we find the cash payment to Lancaster increased to ten marks. Still the disputes continued, and in 1298 an agreement was made that the priory should receive eighteen marks for the great tithes only, while the lesser tithes remained payable to the prior, or to the vicar of Poulton on his behalf. The Stanlaw community had moved to Whalley in 1296 and it may be that this arrangement was intended to create good relations between two religious houses that were now neighbours.

About the same time, Lancaster Priory was in dispute with Furness Abbey over the tithes of the abbey's grange at Beaumont near Lancaster, while another keenly contested dispute with Furness concerned fishing in the River Lune. Furness had fishing rights but was required to render to Lancaster Priory the catch of every third throw of its net. This would have been particularly contentious if the first and second casts were unproductive while the third yielded a heavy catch. Though there is no record of the species of fish concerned, we may suppose that we are dealing here with prime salmon and it is little wonder that in 1314 an exchange of blows is recorded between the Furness fishermen and the servants of the prior of Lancaster.

Sometimes a dispute might be settled by reasoned discussion but occasionally matters took a turn more violent even than that on the Lune. At Poulton, just after Christmas 1330, the prior of Lancaster, together with a number of his servants, was violently abducted by armed men under the direction of Sir Adam Banastre, holder of considerable acreage in the Poulton area. The position of Adam's land meant that access to the fords on the river could only be obtained by crossing his property and since the prior's men had much business in the area they were often required to pass that way when returning to Lancaster. Collection and transportation of tithes, and the driving of beasts, via the Wyre fords required a good deal of activity on the part of the prior's servants and they frequently crossed and re-crossed Adam's land, to the detriment of his crops. Adam protested in vain, and eventually took into his own hands the righting of what had become a major grievance. On Saint Stephen's Day the prior, Ralph Courait, was visiting his tenants at Poulton when he and his servants were seized by armed men and bundled off to Thornton where they were held in rough captivity until at least the feast of the Epiphany, 6 Jan. 1331. So badly were they treated that some were wounded and unable to work for a considerable time. Adam's precipitate action produced the desired result and the prior agreed that his men should be a great deal more circumspect when making their way to the fords thereafter.

As an alien priory the legal status of Lancaster was different from that of other monasteries. In its early days it mattered little that the monks were French and that dues and surplus profits were rendered to the mother-house in Normandy, but later, when Normandy was lost to the English crown and became part of the kingdom of France, the two countries often found themselves at war. French monks, who were enemy aliens sending money and goods across the Channel, could not now be tolerated by the English crown. When England and France first went to war, the lands of an alien house would be sequestered by the crown and rented out to other estates, sometimes to monasteries. In 1360, for example, we find Lancaster's manor of Aldcliffe leased to one John de Ipre at an annual rent of £20, payable to the king. Similarly part of the Lancaster estate passed temporarily into the hands of the abbot of Cockersand, on payment of rent to the king.

By the end of the fourteenth century this situation was no longer acceptable and the position of the alien houses was to be changed for ever. They were summarily taken away from their parent houses with which they were to have no further contact. Many of the larger alien houses became denizen, their connection with the continent severed and their status as English houses assured. Most of the smaller houses, however, including Lancaster, ceased to be monasteries at all and were given, with all their possessions, to other institutions such as colleges, hospitals and religious houses to enhance the wealth of the recipient. Lancaster ceased to be a monastery in 1428 when it was given as a parish church with its various dependent chapels, its lands and entitlements, by Henry V, victor of Agincourt, to the Bridgettine nuns at Syon Abbey in Middlesex.

Lancaster Priory Church, built in the perpendicular style. The present building was constructed mainly after the departure of the Benedictine monks

Lancaster was just one of Syon's many possessions throughout the country. It was managed by agents on behalf of the abbess, while the parish was run by a vicar under the patronage of Syon Abbey. All the spiritualities and temporalities pertaining to the church and parish accrued to Syon. The new holders of the Lancaster estate chose not to retain their right to fish caught in the Lune by the servants of Furness Abbey. Though no longer a monastery in its own right, Lancaster remained a monastic possession for more than a hundred years after 1428.

Syon Abbey had been in existence for little more than a century when it was dissolved along with all the other monastic houses of England. In 1534 the Act of Supremacy was passed, stating that Henry VIII and his successors, not the Pope, were to be Head of the Church of England. This caused immediate problems for the clergy, including monks, and canons in the religious houses, since they were required to take the Oath of Supremacy, thereby accepting both the letter and spirit of the act. Most took the oath, but a number refused, even under threat of the death penalty. A good many priests and monks were actually executed for their stand, including Richard Reynolds, an ordained monk of Syon Abbey.

In 1535 Henry VIII commissioned a survey of all churches and religious establishments in the country, and in particular he required to know the annual income of churches and monasteries alike. This great work, the *Valor Ecclesiasticus*, is valuable in giving us a picture of the economic condition of the individual monasteries at the end of their lifespan. Syon Abbey's net annual income in 1535 was £1,731, well in excess of £580,000 in early twenty-first century terms. This is an income greater than that of any of the Cistercian houses and exceeded by only a handful of the great Benedictine houses. To the end, Syon maintained its religious community at a high numerical level and despite the large number of its nuns granted state pensions, many of them went off to Flanders to join the Bridgettine convent of Dermond.

Their Middlesex house was briefly revived in 1557 under Queen Mary but on her death the sisters again withdrew to the continent. The Syon community is the only English religious body to have remained in continuous existence from the Dissolution to the present day. The nuns went to Portugal after Mary's death and remained there until the middle of the nineteenth century when they returned to England. They are now located at South Brent in Devon.

At Lancaster the property of Syon Abbey was dealt with in much the same way as that of other monasteries. In 1557 the greater part of the estate was sold by the crown to Robert Dalton of Bispham for £1,667. There is little to tell us of the existence there for more than three hundred years of a small Benedictine priory. The site is well known but there are no remains of buildings. The priory church is magnificent and remains in use as the parish church. It is, however, not the building that the French Benedictines of Lancaster Priory would have known. The church we now see is mainly in the perpendicular style and was largely reconstructed under the aegis of Syon Abbey in the fifteenth century. It is 140 feet in length, having undergone much alteration and enlargement. An Anglo-Saxon door in the west wall points to a very early foundation. Lancaster Priory has much to interest us, and the church contains plenty to admire. In particular the exquisitely carved choir-stalls are said to have come from Cockersand Abbey but this has yet to be proved.

Exquisite choir-stalls at Lancaster Priory Church; did they come from Cockersand Abbey?

Porch and door in the Norman style

PENWORTHAM PRIORY,
DEDICATED TO ST. MARY

There is some confusion as to the foundation date of the Benedictine priory of Penwortham, a cell or satellite of Evesham Abbey. The generally accepted date is around 1140 but it is just possible that it was founded some fifty years earlier. This discrepancy arises through the foundation charter of Penwortham, countersigned by the abbot of Evesham. The signature is obscure and may indicate an abbot named Robert. The only Abbot Robert of Evesham held office 1086-96 so if indeed he is the signatory then the early date would apply. However, it is more likely that the signature is that of Abbot Reginald, c.1130-49.

There was certainly a connection at an early date between Evesham and the Penwortham area when Roger of Poitou gave the nearby vill of Howick to the abbey before 1100. It is not surprising then, that Penwortham's founder, Warin Bussel, holder of the barony of Penwortham, whose wife held land in Evesham, and who probably came from Worcestershire, should bestow land and property on this distant abbey. Warin's endowment comprised the church of Penwortham, with all its tithes and other income, the whole township of Farington, and a fourth part of the manor of Great Marton, across the Ribble. He also gave pensions (money paid in lieu of tithes) from the church of Leyland and the chapel of North Meols. Evesham Abbey undertook to send three monks and a secular chaplain to serve Penwortham church, and also to accept Bussel's son Warin, should he wish to become a monk. Bussel's eldest son, Richard, later gave land to

Evesham, together with the advowsons of Leyland and North Meols. The total of land in the Penwortham holding amounted to about 2,500 acres and so we are considering here an establishment of very modest proportion, with an income in 1535 of only £29.

These grants of land and other property were all made to the abbey of Evesham, and not to the priory of Penwortham which remained throughout its life a cell of Evesham with no vestige of independence. The monks were always monks of Evesham and the prior was often referred to as *custos*, which means keeper or watchman, and was intended to emphasise his subordinate status. Occasionally a prior might enter into some transaction but that he was doing so on behalf of the abbey of Evesham was usually made clear in the deed. Penwortham was required to pay to Evesham an annual sum amounting to more than half the priory's income, thus obliging the prior to maintain his own establishment and pay his dues and debts on very little. As Penwortham was not an independent house there is not much of interest recorded, and though it was in existence for around 400 years we know very little about what went on beyond the day to day running of a minor establishment with two or three monks serving nearby churches.

There were, however, a few noteworthy events. From 1330 to 1343 Queen Isabella's steward demanded *puture*: the right for him to be fed and housed together with his attendants during the three weeks court in Penwortham. The sheriff of Lancaster demanded similar hospitality for himself and his servants. Hospitality was one of the  functions of a monastery and many a religious house rang with the jostle of the comings and goings of visitors, rich and poor. Even for major houses, though, there was a limit. The huge Benedictine abbey of Bury St. Edmunds was brought to near bankruptcy in the late fourteenth century when king Richard II and his train descended upon the abbey and stayed for ten days without any payment. We are considering perhaps 100 men here, together with horses, hounds and hawks, and it cost the abbey the staggering sum of 800 marks for less than two weeks. It took a generation to recover. This is an extreme case, but Penwortham Priory faced a proportionate situation. The matter was taken before a jury which found in favour of Penwortham against the dowager queen's steward, and awarded damages, not to the Prior of Penwortham, but to the Abbot of Evesham. Seven years later the claim for *puture* on behalf of the sheriff was also abandoned, doubtless to the relief of the Penwortham monks.

We know little of those who lived at Penwortham Priory. There is a list of priors but most are no more than names. Even when it is apparent that the same man served as prior on two separate occasions we do not know why, though when a great abbey held one or more cells it was not uncommon for the abbot to send difficult or troublesome monks to serve in them as a form of exile. John of Gloucester and Robert Yatton seem to have served two terms but we know little of these men, nor why they were appointed a second time. Prior Ralph of Wilcote also served two terms and we do know a little about him since he left money for the extra feeding of the monks after their periodic blood-letting as prescribed by St. Benedict of Nursia.

There is one individual, however, who stands out from all who ever served at Penwortham. His name was Roger Norris, and there can be few English medieval monks with a reputation so badly tarnished as his. Norris began his monastic life at Canterbury. During his time there the monks, who served the cathedral, were in dispute with Baldwin, Archbishop of Canterbury, over the matter of property such as churches and manors and whether these were the prerogative of the cathedral or the priory. Also, Baldwin, a Cistercian, thought that the life led by the Benedictine monks at Canterbury was far too easy, in sharp contrast with his austere Cistercian upbringing. Roger Norris had

30

no feelings of solidarity with his fellow monks in their dispute with the archbishop and betrayed their plans to Baldwin, who had him appointed prior of the cathedral priory. Norris' treachery was discovered and the monks locked him up in a cell from which he escaped by crawling through a sewer. Not long after his escape, he was removed from his position as prior, but was then appointed Abbot of Evesham, on the insistence of King Richard 'the Lionheart' himself. This is indeed a surprising development. Evesham was one of the largest and wealthiest of Benedictine houses and its abbot held one of the most prestigious of monastic positions in. It was such an important house that it was later to become one of the 'mitred' abbeys whose abbot held a seat in Parliament. To be brought from the disreputable circumstances in which he had placed himself at Canterbury and appointed, by the king, to the abbacy of one of the great Benedictine houses suggests a high degree of influence and possibly family connections.

Norris was abbot of Evesham from 1191 to 1213 and managed during that time to alienate his monks and just about everyone else with whom he had dealings. He is described as: a drunkard, lecher and embezzler who appropriated the abbey's resources to his own use and reduced his monks to near starvation, their garments in rags and lacking shoes for their feet. Despite his many faults Norris was a charmer who could

31

persuade others of his good intentions. He survived revolt by his monks, and enquiries by his superiors. Eventually, in 1213, charged with wasting revenues and property, simony, manslaughter, neglecting to wear monastic attire and gross immorality, he was removed from office.

His character blackened, apparently irrevocably, Norris could still call upon contacts and influence that allowed him yet another appointment. He became Prior of Penwortham in November 1213 and immediately began to display the vices for which he had become notorious. It took only a few months for his conduct to come before the papal legate who removed him from office in April 1214. Even now, the influence that had worked for Roger in the past was still at work. He was re-appointed prior of Penwortham in 1218 and remained there till his death in 1223. The priory, poor and insignificant though it was in good times, was brought to the brink of financial disaster by one of the most immoral and unscrupulous monks ever recorded in medieval England.

The last prior of Penwortham was Richard Hawkesbury who held office from 1515 or 16 to a date some time before 1539. Like Norris, Hawkesbury was accused of immorality, but the evidence against him was much less convincing. He had been appointed by Cardinal Wolsey, who fell from favour and died in disgrace and Hawkesbury was thus a ready target for charges of misconduct. When surveying the monasteries with a view to closing them down and seizing their assets it was an easy matter for the king's commissioners to level unsubstantiated accusations of vice against abbots and priors the better to justify their actions. No proof was necessary; accusation was usually quite sufficient for odium to attach itself to the man and his establishment. It is likely that Prior Hawkesbury was a victim of such underhand tactics.

Like many priory cells, Penwortham was not actually closed by the king's commissioners. Such cells and their associated estates were the property of the mother house, and in an effort to avoid the closure and seizure of their satellites, some of the large houses withdrew their monks and rented out the land and buildings so as to retain possession of them. This course was followed by Evesham in respect of Penwortham at some point after 1535. In the event, it served no purpose since Evesham itself was seized by the crown in 1539 and its properties sold off, including those associated with Penwortham. In February 1539, nine months before the closure of Evesham, the abbot rented the priory or manor and rectory of Penwortham and the rectory of Leyland to John Fleetwood of London, for ninety-nine years at a rent of £99 5s. 3d. The Fleetwoods were a prominent Lancashire family after which a town came to be named some 400 years later. John Fleetwood undertook to repair the chancels of the churches at Penwortham and Leyland and to find a priest to serve at Penwortham now that the monks were gone. Though Evesham Abbey had been seized, Fleetwood continued to hold the lease of Penwortham but now paid his rent to the crown. In January 1543 he purchased the entire Penwortham estate from the crown for the sum of £893 18s. 8d. It remained in his family for more than 200 years, being purchased in 1749 by John Aspinall.

Though there were large numbers of religious houses in medieval England, many of them were, like Penwortham, minor establishments that were in reality little more than a church and a couple of outlying chapels served by two or three monks and supported by a relatively small amount of land in the area. Indeed, it was often the churches that provided a living for the monks, as in the case of Penwortham where the churches of Penwortham and Leyland produced almost all of the priory's income.

We know little of what the priory looked like. It was almost certainly not built on the standard monastic plan around a cloister, but will have consisted of a dormitory or individual chambers for the three or four monks, a refectory and a chapel. We might also suppose some kind of guest accommodation, otherwise there would have been little point in various people demanding puture. The buildings stood a little way to the south of the parish church, in what is now a built-up area where streets have been given such names as: Priory Crescent, Priory Close and Monks' Walk. A major residence was built by the Fleetwood family before 1550, and there stood on the site a mansion or manor house of one kind or another down to the twentieth-century when a large house known as '*Penwortham Priory*' was finally demolished. Nothing now remains of this insignificant satellite of a distant abbey. Like so many of the minor religious houses, its monks, honest, decent men in the main, did their best to serve the local community and are now gone and forgotten. Only a few such as Roger Norris have been recorded.

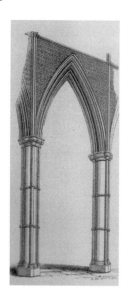

LYTHAM PRIORY,
DEDICATED TO SAINT CUTHBERT

The manor of Lytham is situated on the northern side of the Ribble estuary, midway between Preston and Blackpool, and was the site of the only monastery to have existed for any substantial length of time within the hundred of Amounderness. Lytham is listed in Domesday Book as comprising two carucates, perhaps 240 acres, but its total acreage is 5,309½ acres. The Domesday measurement indicates the area of land said to be in useful production, while the remainder, more than 5,000 acres, was waste, namely moss, salt marsh and blown sand: land of little agricultural use. The manor is one of only a few in the area that can show a pre-Conquest family holding and retaining it beyond the time of the Norman kings. Lord of the manor in 1066 was one Ragnahald, like many in Amounderness evidently of Scandinavian descent. He was succeeded by his son, Ravenkil, his grandson, Roger, and great grandson, Richard who inherited the manor around 1157 and became founder of the Benedictine priory that was to hold it for more than 350 years. It is probable that the 'Ravenkil, son of Ragnald' [sic], who witnessed the founding charter of Lancaster Priory in 1094 is the above-mentioned member of this ancient family.

In the late twelfth century the feudal overlord of Lancashire was John, Count of Mortain, later King John, younger brother of King Richard I. He gave permission for the manor of Lytham to be given to any religious body for the purpose of establishing a monastic house. Richard held the manor *in thegnage* at a rent of 8s. 10d. per annum, and John stipulated that this sum must be paid by the new holders, whoever they might be. Later John showed his good will towards the new religious house by remitting the rent. The intention was to give the church of Lytham, which belonged to Richard's family, to an existing monastery for the abbot or prior of that house to send some of his monks to set up a religious house, run the church and the manor, and live off the income they provided.

Richard entered into discussion on the matter with the abbots of two major Benedictine abbeys: Shrewsbury, at that time holders of the nearby manor of Kirkham, and Evesham, owners of the priory cell at Penwortham, just across the Ribble from Preston. Negotiations with both these houses were clearly well advanced. Hugh, abbot of Shrewsbury, had nominated one of his monks, Robert de Stafford, as head of the projected new house at Lytham, an appointment for which Richard had evidently asked, while Roger Norris, abbot of Evesham, had similarly nominated one of his monks, William, to fill the same post. These negotiations proved abortive, however, and Richard abandoned the idea of an independent house in favour of a cell, established c.1191 and dependent upon the Cathedral Priory of Durham.

Negotiations with Evesham appear to have reached a considerable level of commitment on the part of Richard to the setting up by Evesham of a house at Lytham. In 1243, some fifty years later, we find the abbot and convent of Evesham declaring that their position in Lytham had been usurped by Durham. They referred to their nominee of half a century earlier as William de Lytham, which seems to suggest that he had taken up residence there. Papal officials were involved in seeking a solution to this legal dispute, as they were again in 1272 when Evesham repeated the claim. This time it was finally settled by the payment to Evesham by Durham of 30 marks. Such a conclusion, more than 80 years after the event, suggests that there was more than a little right in Evesham's case. The Worcestershire house had interests in the area much earlier than the date of Lytham Priory's foundation. Penwortham Priory was founded as a cell of Evesham c.1140, though a date as early as c.1090 has been proposed, and it is further suggested that Evesham had a grange at Lytham, which may have been the residence for a time of William de Lytham. Whatever the date of Penwortham's foundation, there will have been Evesham monks living not far from Lytham for at least fifty years before the establishment there of a cell of Durham Cathedral Priory.

Durham has long been associated with Cuthbert, Lytham's patron saint, a native of north-east England who lived c.634-87. The affinity of Lytham with Cuthbert is of ancient date. It is recorded that Richard's grandfather, Ravenkil, pulled down the ancient wattled church and built a new one of stone in honour of Saint Cuthbert. Though Cuthbert is associated with the north east, and has a shrine in Durham Cathedral, he was greatly revered throughout the northern part of the country. In 875, after the destruction by the Vikings, of the abbey of Lindisfarne, where he

37

was buried, a number of the monks took the Saint's remains and relics and travelled around the north of England and south of Scotland, seeking a safe place for them. After an odyssey lasting 120 years the relics were eventually returned to Durham in 995 but it is possible that the monks and their blessed burden may have passed through Lancashire on their travels, and established there a level of devotion to this best-loved of northern saints. There is said to be a stone cross in Lytham marking the spot where the saint's body rested during its travels. Another possible link with the church in north-east England is the story of Kilgrimol Oratory - located about where Saint Annes now stands - and its prior, Oswald the Gentle. It has been suggested that the oratory was built on land in the Lytham area given to Saint Eata, a monk who was a contemporary of Cuthbert, and abbot of a monastery founded at Ripon c.660. Oswald may well have been prior of Kilgrimol at the time when Cuthbert's relics were beginning their peregrinations and would have welcomed their arrival at his church.

A further indicator of a strong Durham connection is the story of Richard's illness that was miraculously cured. Richard was grievously ill and was carried into the church of Saint Cuthbert at Lytham so that he might die there. Immediately upon entering the church his sickness left him and, fully restored to health, he made a pilgrimage to Durham to pray at the shrine of the saint. In the face of a miraculous event such as this it is not surprising that he cut short his negotiations with Shrewsbury and Evesham, and placed his new foundation under the tutelage of a saint who had so clearly demonstrated such care and protection.

Once the monastic foundation at Lytham was established it attracted, in the form of land and tithes, further modest benefactions from local landholders. There were ninety grants of land in nearby townships, namely: Warton, Freckleton, Bilsborrow, Whittingham, Bispham, Bryning, Hawes, Kellamergh, Kirkham, Layton, Marton, Preston and Upper Rawcliffe. These, however, did not amount to 1,000 acres and the total held by the priory, including Lytham itself was a little over 6,242 acres. Though this may appear a fairly impressive estate for a small monastery, the quality of most of the land was so poor that it was barely sufficient to maintain a reasonable level of subsistence for the monks.

The original documents confirming these donations are still in existence. They are the property of Durham Cathedral and are kept in the University of Durham Library, but have never been published. William Farrer, editor of the Cockersand Chartulary, and co-editor of the Victoria County History of Lancashire, transcribed the charters and intended to publish them in the early twentieth century as he had done with those of Cockersand Abbey. He was not able to do so, however, and in 1922 his widow presented his papers to the Manchester Central Library.

Lytham Priory was attended by much difficulty and contention. There were often poor relations with neighbouring landowners, and grazing rights were in dispute with at least three of them: the Butlers of Lytham, the Beethams of Bryning and the Cliftons of Westby. In 1320, William de Clifton is said to have invaded the priory with 200 armed men, rescued some impounded cattle, done damage to the value of £100, and put the prior, Roger of Tynemouth, *"in fear of his life so that he dare not stir abroad."* As late as 1530 we find the Boteler (Butler) family violently asserting its claim to a section of land held by the monks. The Butler men threw down an ancient boundary cross, another cross and a statue of Saint Cuthbert, and threatened the priory itself. They were restrained only when two of the monks brought out the Blessed Sacrament, in honour of which the Butlers and their men desisted.

The revenues of the priory were often at a low ebb. With such poor land at its disposal this is not surprising, though in 1292, Scottish raids were said to be the reason for the poor financial state. Another constant problem was the state of relations with the mother-house at Durham. Some of the Lytham priors resented their complete subordination to the prior of Durham and being subject to instant recall at his behest. Around 1361 prior Robert Kelloe of Lytham objected strongly to being recalled to Durham and went so far as to obtain a papal bull exempting him from removal without good cause being shown. This did not help, however, and he was duly obliged to return to the mother-house. Kelloe was perhaps not a shining example of monastic virtue. In 1355, around the middle of his sojourn of ten or so years at Lytham, he was accused of carrying away goods to the value of £27 from Coldingham Priory, in Berwickshire, when resident there before moving to Lytham. He was also accused of adultery. These were grave charges and just the kind to level at a subordinate prior when his removal was desired. Though he did go back to Durham we do not know if his guilt was ever established.

In 1441, Prior William Patrick was ordered back to Durham but went about defending his position much more strongly than Kelloe had done. First he obtained a papal bull, and then royal letters patent. His position appeared a strong one but the prior of Durham nonetheless found a loophole. He sent a letter to Patrick accusing him of failing to attend general chapter at Durham, and of failing to pay his contribution to the mother-house for the past two years. The prior of Lytham had evidently received

advance warning of this letter since he sent out a band of armed men to intercept the bearer who was seized and threatened that he would be forced to eat the letter he was carrying, '*cum pixede*,' (with pitch). Duly charged with these further offences, Patrick was removed from office.

As a small and poor house that was very much the property of a distant, grand establishment, Lytham did not have numbers of churches and chapels appropriated to it. There was only one distant church given to the monks of Lytham, but this, like so much else in the life of Lytham Priory, turned out to be a problem. Early in the thirteenth century, Margaret, widow of Richard, founder of Lytham Priory, gave the church of Appleby, Leicestershire to the Lytham monks. Welcome though such a gift would normally have been, it became simply another bone of contention. The gift of the church was challenged by two Leicestershire families, the Applebys and the Vernons, and the dispute dragged on for almost three centuries before finally being settled around 1493 by an agreement that ceded patronage of the church of Appleby to the Vernon family in return for an annual payment of one mark (13s. 4d.) from the church to Lytham Priory.

Throughout its existence, Lytham Priory struggled to maintain itself in the face of strained relations with the mother-house, disputes with neighbours, raids by marauding Scots, bad management, poor land and even the loss of an area of reasonable land when a storm covered it with blown sand. Its income in 1535 is recorded as £48 which makes it the second poorest house in the county.

Among the many surviving Lytham documents are numerous *compotus* rolls (accounts). These give a clear picture of the precarious nature of Lytham's finances. That for 1461 is typical. It begins with a list of rents received that year in respect of land in Lytham, Mythop, Eastholme (within Lytham), Bankhouse (within Lytham), Warton, Freckleton, Kellamergh, Carleton,

Rawcliffe, Whittingham and Bilsborrow. These amount to £35 10s. 8½d., which represents almost 63% of receipts. The accounts show very clearly the economic structure of a small Benedictine priory/cell run as a manor by its prior on the basis of some land held in demesne, with the greater part rented out, and further provided for by the revenue of its church and also the dues and charges of a manor.

The list of items in the document commences with the rents indicated above, then reads as follows:

40s. from mills; 18p. *de communi thoralli ville* (from the common oven of the town); 25s. from brewing; 8s. from *gressums* (customary manorial payments and fines); 9s. from summer and winter *agistments* (rented pastures); nothing from the perquisites of the (manorial) court; 12s. from herbage-pasture; 10s. from tithe hay; 26s. from hides of oxen and wool and skins of sheep; 12s. for tithe of flax and hemp; 23s. 4d. for altarage (surplice fees and other minor dues), oblations (donations) and mortuaries (tax payable to the church on the death of an individual); 4d. for anchorage; 3s. for milk; 33s. 4d. for wreck of the sea (flotsam and jetsam found on the shore which became the property of the lord of the manor) + 20s. omitted in last account; 33s. for wool sold; £3 8s. for wheat, barley and peas sold. Sum £56 8s. 10½d. Expenses for year £55 5s. 4d. Balance for year £1 3s. 6½d.

It is of interest to note the variety of the priory's sources of income, small though they all are. Its location on the coast is clearly shown by the entries concerning anchorage and wreck of the sea, but only one entry indicates that this is an account from a religious house, namely that dealing with altarage, oblations and mortuaries. All the other entries could be found in the accounts of any secular Lancashire manor. More interesting, and more alarming is the paucity of cash in the annual balance which

42

represents about £500 pounds in the early twenty-first century. Obliged to eke out a living from such sources as the sale of milk and the fees payable for baking bread, it is little wonder that successive priors of Lytham found difficulty in paying their way.

The end for Lytham Priory came a little earlier than for most of the Lancashire houses. The Oath of Supremacy, requiring monks throughout the country to acknowledge Henry VIII, and not the pope, as head of the church, demonstrated to them the fragile nature of their position, since monks in some parts of England had been executed for refusing to take it, and when the *Valor Ecclesiasticus* was taken in 1535 it was clear to all that the age of the monastery was coming to a close. Probably with this very much in mind, the prior of Durham withdrew his monks from Lytham and rented out the estate. If monasteries were to be closed, then at least the Lytham property might continue to provide revenue for Durham cathedral. Such was not to be the case, however. At a date between 1535 and 1540 the property of Lytham Priory was seized by the crown and let to Thomas Dannet for 80 years at a rent of £48 19s. 6d. Dannet paid his rent to the crown until 1554 when Queen Mary transferred the property to Sir Thomas Holcroft, a man who was to obtain a great deal of former monastic land.

There are no traces of the priory buildings at Lytham, or the stone church built by Ravenkil in honour of Saint Cuthbert. The site is generally held to have been near the elegant eighteenth-century Lytham Hall.

There exists a list of priors, sometimes referred to as '*wardens*,' a term intended to emphasise their status as subordinate to the prior of Durham.

UPHOLLAND PRIORY,
DEDICATED TO ST. THOMAS THE MARTYR

Upholland Priory was the last of the Lancashire monasteries to be founded, and though small, it was the largest of the four Benedictine houses in the county. It was also the only house of that order that was not a satellite of some other, larger house. The founder was Sir Robert de Holland who in 1310 established a college of secular canons on his land four miles west of Wigan. The area was evidently not to the liking of the canons, who deserted the place. Bishop Langton of Lichfield, on finding that the canons were gone, felt that such a wild spot was better suited to monks than to secular clergy and so he obtained Sir Robert's consent to the bringing in of Benedictines and the transfer to them of Sir Robert's original endowments made to the secular canons. This he did in 1319. It is not known from which monastery the newly arrived Benedictines came, but the community consisted of a prior and twelve monks, the customary founding group, intended to represent Christ and his twelve apostles.

There is little recorded about the life of the monks and their affairs within the priory and the neighbourhood. The landholdings of Upholland were small and the annual income was barely sufficient to keep the monks, their employees and the few persons living there on the charity of the house. The endowments consisted of a moiety of the manor of Upholland together with the churches of Childwall near Liverpool and Whitwick near Loughborough, Leicestershire. The priory's holding at Upholland would have been around 2,350 acres but much of this was of poor quality and not under cultivation, though it evidently provided rough pasture. By the time the priory of Upholland had come into being, the practice of renting out monastic estates had begun, and most houses retained only a relatively small part of their estate as demesne land to provide food for themselves. At Upholland the monks retained 54 acres which produced an income of barely £5 a year. No attempt was made to grow wheat, which did not thrive in the boggy soil of Lancashire, and only a few acres of barley and oats were produced. Livestock, particularly cattle, was more appropriate. The Lancashire climate made for abundant grass, and dairy produce was the major part of the priory's output and economy. At the time of the Dissolution, Upholland had 45 cattle and 73 sheep, which together made the priory a considerable producer of cheese.

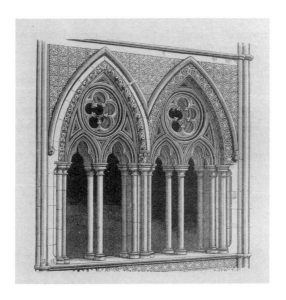

Monasteries often had possessions in far away parts of the country, as we see at Upholland with its appropriated church at Whitwick in Leicestershire, and disputes or litigation were often carried on between parties at great distance from each other. At Whitwick, the priory was in dispute with Henry Tebbe who was liable for payment of tithe to the local church, and thereby to Upholland Priory. He refused to pay, and when prior Robert Fazakerly confronted him during a visit to Whitwick, Tebbe drove him out of the church and threatened him with death if he were to return. The sheriff of Leicestershire failed to help and the prior took the matter before Parliament. Tebbe was arrested and locked in the Fleet prison until he should pay his tithe. He duly paid and obtained his release. Such actions as this were common in medieval England.

At the end of the fifteenth century it was reported to Bishop Hales of Lichfield that the monks of Upholland were not observing the Benedictine rule, that their church was out of repair, their other buildings ruinous and their spiritual and temporal goods dissipated by their negligence. By 1536, however, the buildings were evidently in a good state of repair. As a house with an income of less than £200, Upholland Priory was closed under the Act of Suppression of March 1536 which provided for the closure of all houses with an annual income below that sum.

At the time of its closure, Upholland had only five monks in residence, one of whom was the prior. All were ordained priests and three wished to continue in the monastic life while the other two sought pensions. The monks followed a somewhat relaxed lifestyle, and according to the two Royal Commissioners who visited, Drs Layton and Legh, the prior and two of his brethren were men of exceedingly loose morals. The monks occupied separate bedchambers and lay on feather beds: practices not prescribed in the Benedictine Rule. However, we should, perhaps, be a little suspicious of what Layton, Legh and the other commissioners had to say about the morals and practices in the houses they visited. It was, as we have seen, their business to bring the monasteries to an end and the more lurid the picture they painted the easier would be their task.

Despite the low income of the house, charity was not neglected. At the time of closure there were two aged persons resident and two children at school, all paid for from Upholland's meagre income.

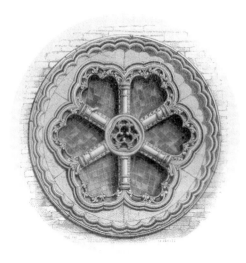

Like many monasteries, Upholland had in its possession relics of saints by which it hoped to attract visitors, if not pilgrims, who would contribute to the priory's income. There were two bones of the upper arm, each held in a silver reliquary; one said to be of St. Thomas of Canterbury, the other of St. Richard of Chichester. Unfortunately for a Lancashire monastery, the area was so poor and underpopulated that even a relic of the venerated Thomas Becket could do little to enhance the financial standing of a house always on the edge of penury. When the house was valued, together with its contents, by three Lancashire knights, Sir William Leyland, Sir Richard Ashton and Sir Thomas Halsall, with Thomas Burgon as auditor and Thomas Armer as receiver, the two reliquaries were valued together at £16 13s. 4d., the not inconsiderable sum in 2006 of around £5,500. Interestingly, the reliquaries, together with a silver chalice valued at £6 13s.4d. were not at the priory but at Gawsworth Hall where Sir Richard Fitton had received them as security for a loan of £10 he had made to the priory. Missing altogether was a pair of gilt salt-cellars given for safe keeping by Elizabeth Bradshaw, brewer and day-woman of the priory to William Topping, servant of the house. Topping could not produce the items when required to do so, and he and his wife were remanded in custody at Lancaster Castle to await trial. Unfortunately we are not informed of the outcome.

At the time of its closure in May 1536, Upholland Priory's net annual income was £53 3s.4d. the greater part of which, £38 13s. 4d. came from the church of Childwall. The bells and lead were valued at £18 and the painted glass in the church was sold for £13, while the church itself, though built for the priory in the fourteenth century, was transferred to local use as a parochial chapel. The total valuation of movables in the church and other buildings, together with livestock, corn etc., plus debts owed to the priory, came to only £114 2s. 8d., while the prior's debts amounted to £18 18s. 10d. The whole was granted by the crown in 1545 to John Holcroft, whose family received huge quantities of monastic property in Lancashire.

The church built for the priory in the fourteenth century survives in part, the chancel of the priory church being the nave of the present parish church. The chancel of the present church was added in the nineteenth century. There are said to be traces of the priory buildings among the houses to the south of the church. After more than 200 years of fairly undistinguished existence, Upholland Priory was no more. It had come and gone without causing too much of a stir in local or national affairs, and yet it had provided services spiritual and temporal to untold numbers of South Lancashire residents that would otherwise never have been available to them. Upholland Priory was not, in fact, the last religious house to stand within the manor. In the nineteenth-century, the restored Catholic Church created there a seminary through which passed large numbers of young men destined for ordination to the priesthood, and many of its alumni are still serving in parishes throughout the country.

KERSAL CELL,
DEDICATED TO SAINT LEONARD

By far the smallest monastic establishment in Lancashire was the Cluniac cell at Kersal, Salford. It stood in the township of Broughton close to the River Irwell and was a satellite of the large Cluniac priory of Lenton, Nottinghamshire. Donor of the site was Stephen Ranulf Gernons, earl of Chester, who gave to Lenton, at a date between 1143 and 53, a portion of his manor of Salford together with the hamlet of Kersal. The area of land was small, amounting in the fourteenth century to 100 acres of arable, 24 acres of meadow and 40 acres of wood, together with three messuages. There was the right to pasture on the waste and to bring it into cultivation, together with fishery rights in the Irwell. These holdings were increased around 1200 by grants of two parcels of land in Ashton-under-Lyne, a parcel of land in Audenshaw to the east of Manchester, and half of Polden in Oldham parish to the north east.

Lenton was, at its inception, an *'alien'* house (see Lancaster Priory), and so its cell at Kersal was alien also. In 1392 Lenton became *'denizen'* (naturalised), a step taken by all the English Cluniac houses shortly before or after that date. This effectively meant that Kersal became denizen at the same time.

There is less recorded on the history of Kersal than on any other Lancashire house. Lenton kept one monk there, sometimes two, and for a short time evidently, three. A small chapel was built on its land, together with accommodation for the monks who lived there. These monks said Mass daily and began to acquire a reputation for piety that attracted local people to services. Around 1200 Albert de Nevill, rector of Manchester complained that the rights of the parish church were being usurped by Kersal in that people were seeking burial at the chapel there and paying their funeral dues to the monks. An agreement was made between the two parties to the effect that parishioners of Manchester might choose to be buried at Kersal but all appropriate dues were to be paid to Manchester parish church, in return for which Kersal was to make to the church an annual gift of two 1½ pound candles of wax. The nature of the relationship here between parish church and monastic cell is amply demonstrated in a provision of the agreement to the effect that no Manchester parishioners were to receive the sacraments at the cell's chapel.

When the king's commissioners, Layton and Legh, visited the cell in 1535 they commented only on financial matters pertaining to it. As a possession of Lenton its fate would be bound up with that of its mother-house. Lenton was closed in 1538 with all the bloodshed and acrimony that we find in so many of these actions. The prior, Nicholas Heath, resisted the closure of the house and was executed for high treason along with two of his monks, Ralph Swenson and William Gylham, together with four labourers. The remaining twenty two monks, together with five elderly men living in the monastery on charity, were summarily turned out onto the street without pensions or any means of providing for themselves. What became of the one or two monks resident at Kersal we do not know. They were evidently not executed but presumably they were turned out in the same manner as their brethren.

In the valuation made in 1535 the annual income of Kersal cell was said to be £9 6s. 8d. The site and lands were leased in1539 for twenty-one years to John Wood, one of the oistryngers, at a rent of £11 6s. 8d. The following year the crown sold the cell to Baldwin Willoughby for £155 6s. 8d.

There is only one mention of a prior. This occurs in 1332, presumably at a time when there were three monks in residence. His name was John of Ingleby.

Nothing remains of the chapel or associated buildings but the site is now occupied by a house known as '*Kersal Cell*', a half-timbered and brick building once occupied by Dr. John Byrom, writer of the hymn, '*Christians Awake, Salute the Happy Morn*', a fitting tribute to the pious monks who once slept here. The house was built by Baldwin Willoughby in the sixteenth-century, and is perhaps the only English house to incorporate the word '*cell*' in its name.

CONISHEAD PRIORY,
DEDICATED TO THE BLESSED VIRGIN MARY

Conishead Priory stood in the Furness peninsula, a little to the south-east of Ulverston and barely eight miles from the great Cistercian house of Furness Abbey. The original foundation was c.1154 when a hospital was established for lepers and poor persons. The setting up of a priory may have been in the founder's mind but it is easy to see how he might have been deterred from doing so by the proximity of the powerful Furness Abbey.

Despite the nearness of such a neighbour, the decision to set up an Augustinian priory was taken in 1181, or earlier, by Gamel de Pennington, holder of the manor of Ulverston. It is also suggested, that the founder might have been William de Lancaster II, baron of Kendal. Certainly William was an early benefactor who gave to the new priory: all the vill of Conishead, the church of Ulverston, 40 acres of land in Ulverston, and salt-workings, turbary, pasture, pannage and timber-taking in his wood of Furness and manor of Ulverston. The charter of William de Lancaster is a little ambiguous, however, and the historian William Farrer has suggested that he was merely confirming the gift of Conishead as Gamel de Pennington's feudal superior.

Subsequent benefactions lay mainly in Furness, the district of Copeland in Cumberland, and in Westmorland. William of Lancaster III extended the priory's landholding in Ulverston, and he also gave to the canons fishing rights in Coniston Water and in the rivers Crake and Leven. These were of great value: the Crake empties Coniston into the Leven, and the Leven empties Windermere into Morecambe Bay. Further land was given at Bardsey, a little to the south of Conishead, and in Torver, west of Coniston Water, also in Copeland at Whitbeck, and at Hale. In Westmorland the priory was given the hospital of Kendal, or Scalthwaiterigg, and Baysbrown in Great Langdale, not far from

Elterwater, a moiety of the vill of Patton, north east of Kendal and the manor of Haverbrack in Beetham, south of Milnthorpe.

In addition, Conishead Priory held seven churches and the chapel of Drigg, near Ravenglass. These churches, as with those of most of the other small Lancashire monasteries, brought in a greater income than did their landholdings. The churches in question were: Pennington and Ulverston in Furness, Muncaster, Whitbeck, Ponsonby and Hale in Cumberland, and Orton in Westmorland. Conishead is situate in Furness and it is clear that the influence of the powerful Furness Abbey led to the priory's receiving most of its benefactions in Cumberland and Westmorland, as far away from its large neighbour as possible.

There were a few disputes between Conishead Priory and Furness Abbey, mainly concerning the church of Hawkeshead, which both claimed. The matter was finally settled on amicable terms, the priory paying to the abbey a pension of £6 per annum. Other conditions governing the relationship between the two houses required that the number of canons at Conishead should not exceed thirteen, no woman should reside in the priory, and any land that the priory might obtain in Furness was to be confined to the Ulverston fief. Furness was not the only abbey to be in dispute, however. A little after 1300 the abbot of Whitby laid claim to Orton church, declaring it to be a chapel of the church of Crosby Ravensworth, held by Whitby. In 1309 the abbot seized Orton church by force and held it until the following year, when he agreed to arbitration, the outcome of which was that church must be returned permanently to Conishead Priory. As with many houses of canons regular, the prior appointed one of his own canons as vicar.

On the whole, Conishead's record of litigation is quite modest, but religious houses were always at risk from individuals seeking to gain some advantage, or from other religious houses with similar motives. In 1440 Sir Thomas Parr of Kendal claimed the priory's right to Saint Leonard's Hospital, or leprosarium, in the town and the canons were obliged to go to law in order to recover it. The Parrs were a notable Kendal family, a member of which, Katherine, was to become the sixth and last wife of Henry VIII 100 years later.

In 1525 Conishead Priory was threatened with closure, more than a decade before such a fate became reality for all the English monasteries. Between 1524 and 29, Cardinal Wolsey, the most powerful man in the English church, and second only to the king in matters of state, obtained papal and royal authority for the closure of twenty-nine houses of monks, canons and nuns. His purpose was to take the combined assets of these houses and use them to found a college at Oxford, to be called Cardinal College in his own memory. He also intended to set up a college in Ipswich, the town from which he had come, the son of a butcher. The rest of the houses earmarked for closure were duly taken by Wolsey. Conishead, however, was saved from closure at the eleventh hour by the duke of Suffolk who intervened to declare that: '*the house is of great succour to the King's subjects, and the prior, George Carnforth, of virtuous disposition.*' The support of the duke deferred closure for a little over ten years, but for Wolsey, time had almost run out. A sick man, he fell from favour in 1529. His Ipswich college was never built and he died at Leicester Abbey in 1530. The name of his new college at Oxford was changed to its present title, Christ Church College.

The next prior of Conishead, Thomas Lord, was also the last, and he did not enjoy the kind of approbation afforded his predecessor by the duke of Suffolk. After the death of Wolsey, the king had turned increasingly to Thomas Cromwell as his chief instrument both in the devising and the implementing of policy,

54

and Cromwell gathered about him a group of henchmen who were to oversee the destruction of England's monasteries between 1535 and 1540. Chief among these were Doctors Legh and Layton, lawyers both, who went about the business of subverting the religious houses with ruthlessness and cynicism. In 1533 Thomas Legh wrote to Cromwell alleging that the prior of Conishead had contrived the murder of John Bardsey, Legh's cousin, in circumstances of great barbarity. Though the allegation was brought before Mr Justice Fitz Herbert at Lancaster assizes, no indictment was made for lack of any motive or evidence. John Bardsey had undoubtedly been murdered, but there was nothing to suggest that Prior Lord had anything to do with it. The only other allegation was made by Richard Johnson who had worked as guide to those crossing the Leven sands as an employee of the priory. Johnson said that the prior had maliciously dismissed him from his post because he had arrested Edward Lancaster for the murder of John Bardsey, and that Lancaster had committed the crime at the behest of Prior Lord.

With these unhappy events very much in the air, Conishead Priory faced the ordeal that every single monastic house in England had to endure about that time: a visitation from the King's commissioners acting under the orders of Thomas Cromwell, ostensibly to assess the financial and moral circumstances of the house and its inmates, and also a visit from a group of auditors to value the house and its possessions. Again the commissioners were Doctors Layton and Legh who conducted their enquiry with their accustomed cynicism. There were eight canons in residence, including the prior, together with the retired prior, George Carnforth, living in the priory as a pensioner. There was one more canon belonging to the house but he was acting as vicar at Orton church. The former prior and the vicar of Orton desired to be released from their monastic vows. According to Layton and Legh, five of the canons were guilty of sexual incontinence, two in aggravated form. They did not specify the nature of the offence, however, and what they reported is typical of what they had to say in respect of monks and canons up and down the country. Given that Cromwell's purpose was the closure of the monasteries it was the task of Legh, Layton and the other commissioners to return reports that would totally justify such an outcome.

The audit and valuation were conducted by a group of Lancashire knights and gentlemen charged with putting a value on anything and everything at the priory. These men were: Sir Marmaduke Tunstall, Sir James Leybourne, Thomas Shirbourne, squire, Thomas Burgoyne, auditor, and Thomas Armer, receiver. This group found the church and buildings in good condition with two persons, one a widow, living there on charity. There were nine servants and fourteen officers of the household together with sixteen farmworkers and others employed outdoors. When the priory closed, the prior was to be provided for by the vicarage of Orton while each of the other canons was to receive a pension of £1 17s. 8d.

The annual income of the house in 1535 was assessed at £97, though the commissioners later raised this figure to £161 5s. 9d. The lead from the flashings and guttering was valued, together with the bells, at £44 18s. 0d, and moveable goods of all kinds such as furniture, choir stalls, cooking equipment and window glass were said to be worth a total of £288, while the priory had outstanding debts of a little under £88.

At many of the defunct English monasteries we can see the personal interest of the officials in bringing about the closure of the house in that one or other of them bought, or tried to buy, all or part of the property. In the case of Conishead, Thomas Burgoyn the auditor negotiated the purchase of the priory site and some of the other land but the deal was never finalised, the property going instead to Sir William Paget.

There is nothing now to be seen of the Augustinian priory of Conishead. A large house was built on the site in the nineteenth century and the priory church was said to have been discovered to the south of it, the north transept being under the present house.

Fine Norman door with '*blind*' arches beginning to show the transition to the Early English style

CARTMEL PRIORY
DEDICATED TO ST. MARY: OUR LADY OF CARTMEL

Cartmel Priory, a house of Augustinian canons, was founded around 1190 by William Marshal, Earl of Pembroke. The initial endowment was the whole of the Cartmel district between the rivers Leven and Winster. This is a substantial and clearly demarcated area, with the Leven reaching the waters of Morecambe Bay above Greenodd, and the Winster a little to the east of Grange over Sands. It was granted to Marshal by Henry II in 1185-6. Included in the endowment was the parish church of Cartmel with its dependent chapels. The founding colony of canons came from the substantial priory of Bradenstoke in Wiltshire, but the charter excluded any dependence on the mother-house. The old church of Saint Michael at Cartmel was demolished, with the consent of the diocesan bishop, and replaced by the new priory church dedicated to Saint Mary, Our Lady of Cartmel. An altar to Saint Michael was reserved in the new church for the use of the parishioners and served by one of the canons, or a secular priest appointed by the prior. Such an arrangement: the priory within the town and the canons serving the local community as parish clergy, preachers, teachers and providers of a variety of services may be seen as the ideal for an Augustinian house.

The fief of Cartmel, with which the priory had been endowed by the founder, was a compact area, readily governable by the prior and canons. This control was made complete by the founder's granting to the canons all the seigniorial powers and privileges he had up to that time himself enjoyed. John confirmed these privileges to the priory on his becoming king in 1199. It is worth detailing the list as it is one of the most comprehensive catalogues of immunities to be found in the fee of a medieval religious house. They include: sac and soc; toll and team; ingfangenthef and outfangenthef; freedom of suit to the shire or hundred courts; exemption from pleas of murder, theft, hamsoken and forestel;

from scutage, geld, danegeld, dona, scots and aids; from toll, tallage, lastage and pontage; from castle-work and bridge-work, and from all other customs and secular exactions. This solid, clearly demarcated block of land, with its rights and privileges so carefully defined, made Cartmel Priory and its estate the archetypal feudal holding, with the prior exercising the powers of a baron on his own demesne.

Cartmel Priory Church with its unusual angled upper-tower

There were other rights and privileges claimed by the priory in the Cartmel area that were in fact withheld by the crown and bestowed upon others. For example, the prior claimed the right to wreck of the sea and to waif judgement but these were denied him by the crown and given to Edmund, Earl of Lancaster. The holding of the sheriff's tourn, a responsibility that would normally have devolved upon the local baron or lord of the manor, was disclaimed by the priory. (The tourn was the visit by the sheriff to various parts of his jurisdiction, on a tour of inspection and for the holding of court.) Arrangements were usually made by the local lords, and hospitality provided for the sheriff and his train. It is a clear indication of the favour in which the priory was held that the canons were able to renounce this expensive feudal responsibility.

In addition to the priory's holding in Cartmel, the canons received from William Marshal a number of properties on his Irish estates. These lands, the extensive Clare estates in Leinster, had come to Marshal through his marriage in 1189 to Isabel, daughter and heiress of Richard of Clare (known as 'Strongbow'). He gave to the canons of Cartmel the vill of Kilrush in Kildare, also the advowson of its church, together with the church of Ballysax and the chapel of Ballymaden in the diocese of Kildare. There was also land belonging to Cartmel at Callan in Tipperary. The priory's principal Irish holding was Kilrush, where a survey of 1536-7 shows the Cartmel canons in possession of 360 acres of land, of which 60 had lain uncultivated for some time. The remaining 300 acres were said to be worth 12d. an acre and were held by six tenants who paid a total of £15 per year. There were eleven cottagers on the estate who paid no rent but were required to perform two days of work in the autumn, and at Christmas all tenants were bound to provide a cockerel, valued at 2d.. The manor of Kilrush produced for Cartmel Priory the annual sum of £16 4s. 6d. In addition the church produced 66s. 2d. in tithes, and 20s. altarage, together with10s.from a water mill and 2s.from a dovecote. The total value of the church was £6 6s. 8d., giving a total from manor and church of £22 11s. 2d. The income from these possessions was not counted along with that from the Cartmel fief, and the priory was therefore considerably better endowed than appearances might have suggested. These Irish possessions necessitated frequent visits by canons from Cartmel, which led to an arrangement with the Augustinian prior and convent of the cathedral church of Holy Trinity in Dublin that any canon visiting from Cartmel should be entertained and treated as one of their own..

The first half-century or so of Cartmel priory's existence was not altogether peaceful. Perhaps because of the absence in

60

Ireland of various canons, there was a good deal of unrest that led to intervention by Pope Innocent IV, 1243-54. It was revealed that there had been disobedience to the prior, cases of personal violence by canons to other members of the house, and canons retaining private property in direct contravention of the Rule of St. Augustine. These offences led to the excommunication of a number of canons and lay-brothers, and to some of the excommunicated canons celebrating mass and the sacraments while still un-absolved. In 1245 the same pope gave authority for the prior to absolve those who were penitent, provided their offences had not been too serious, and to suspend for two years those who remained obstinate. Any found guilty of violence were to be sent to the pope himself for absolution. The discontent at Cartmel evidently continued, and in 1248 the archbishop of York commissioned the abbot of Furness and the precentor of Beverley to investigate the state of affairs and, if they thought it appropriate, to remove the prior and his subordinates from office.

Cartmel's geographical position made it highly vulnerable to armed incursion from Scotland, whether by Scottish royal armies in time of formally declared war, or by armed raiders who were freebooters acting on their own behalf. This was particularly the case during the years following Robert Bruce's defeat of Edward II at the battle of Bannockburn in 1314. For example, in 1319 Bruce, while holding Berwick against an English army, detached a  substantial force under Sir James Douglas to raid southward into Yorkshire. On 20 September it met, at Mitton in Swaledale, a hastily gathered Yorkshire force of priests, monks, farmers and townsmen under the archbishop of York. Such a gathering was no match for the Scots and was badly cut up, the survivors harried in all directions, and the archbishop barely escaping with his life.

The immediate outcome was the total vulnerability of towns, estates and religious houses in the north of England. Sawley Abbey suffered particularly heavily from the depredations of the victorious Scots. In 1316 and 1322 there were Scottish raids so severe on Cartmel and its estates that its valuation fell from £46 13s. 4d. to £8.

Around 1390, complaints were made about the prior, William Lawrence, who was said to have been guilty of *'serious misconduct'*. His alleged misdeeds came to the attention of Pope Boniface IX who ordered an enquiry. Lawrence, who had become prior in 1381, was accused of *'dilapidations'*, that is, knowingly allowing the buildings to fall into disrepair, *'simony'* in that he charged a fee to those applying to become canons of Cartmel and of spending the proceeds in depraved uses and frequent visits to taverns. As suggested by the accusation of dilapidation, the buildings were said to be ruinous, divine service and hospitality neglected, and great scandal caused by the prior's mode of life. The archbishop of York was ordered to deprive Prior Lawrence of his position and arrange for the election of a new prior, though this does not appear to have happened since Lawrence was still in office five years later.

The records of Cartmel Priory are virtually blank for the fifteenth-century. There is also a gap in the list of priors, which suggests that documents have been lost. At the very end of the century we find reference to an appeal by prior William Hale to Pope Alexander VI against his removal from office and the sequestration of the priory's revenues by Christopher Urswick, archdeacon of Richmond from 1494 to 1500. Hale declared that the charges of certain, unspecified, 'excesses' were falsely brought. The Pope ordered an enquiry, but the outcome has not been preserved. It would seem that prior Hale was vindicated for he was still in office in 1501, when he appealed to the Archbishop of York to order the return to Cartmel of two canons, Miles Burre and William Payne, who had left the house without permission

62

and taken up secular disputes. It may be supposed that Miles Burre, at least, returned with due penitence, since in 1504 we find him as prior of Cartmel.

Though we know little of what took place at Cartmel during the fifteenth-century, we might suppose that, despite reports of misdeeds by priors and canons, the house was growing in prosperity, and that there was an increase in vocations to the contemplative life. After the Black Death in the middle of the fourteenth-century we find, for obvious reasons, a serious decline in numbers of religious throughout the country. This situation was rectified only slowly in the fifteenth-century, but during the reign of Henry VII, (1485-1509) we see in many houses a significant increase in the numbers of monks and canons. There were also new building projects being undertaken in what was a period of growth and confidence. This is evident in the towers being built on the churches of a number of monasteries in the north of England. Furness, Holm Cultram Abbey, Shap Abbey, Bolton Priory and others, display visible evidence of west towers, though some were started but never completed. At Cartmel this new-found monastic confidence and prosperity under the earlier Tudors manifested itself in the building, in 1504, of a chapel at Cartmel Fell, six miles from the priory. Residents of that district had been obliged to travel to the priory church to attend mass and the sacraments, and at this date the prior, probably the Miles Burre referred to above as a defaulter, decided to build a chapel where services could be provided for these outlying farming families. The chapel, still in use today, is a fine example of

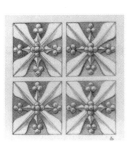

vernacular architecture. The interior is that of a heavily beamed structure like a Lake District barn with an air of permanence about it, an irony that its builders could not have recognised since they were not to know that, within the lifetime of some of them, Cartmel Priory, and all the other monasteries, would be gone.

In 1535 the income of Cartmel was assessed at £91 6s. 3d., a figure increased by the commissioners the following year to £212 12s. 10½d. Parliament ordered, in 1536, that all religious houses with fewer than twelve inmates and an income below £200 were to be closed, and the Lancashire knights who came to act as the king's commissioners, falsely increased the stated income in the hope of saving the priory, or at least postponing its demise.

The commissioners who came to Cartmel were those who visited Conishead, namely: Sir Marmaduke Tunstall, Sir James Leybourne, Thomas Shirbourne, Squire, Thomas Burgoyne, Auditor, and Thomas Armer, Receiver. The commissioners at Cartmel, and those who visited every other religious house in the country were obliged to place a value on goods and chattels and everything moveable, and therefore saleable. With the expectation that buildings were to be demolished, they placed a value of £15 10s. 4d. on lead flashings and guttering, together with the bells. Moveable goods were assessed at £185 14s. 5½d., plate £27 3s. 1½d., church ornaments £9 6s. 8d., window glass and iron window bars £12 19s., cattle £73 6s. 8d., household linen and implements £18 13s. 5d., and corn in store £54 5s. 8d.

At this critical time in the life of Cartmel Priory there were ten canons belonging to the house. Of these, two were said to be guilty of incontinence, one of them having six children. Richard Preston, the prior, aged forty-one, was one of them, the other being William Panell who was 68 years old, had licence from the convent to live wherever he chose, and had also been given a pension of £5 13s. 4d., although this had been taken from him by Doctors Legh and Layton. The other eight were priests of good standing: James Eskerige aged 36, John Ridley 32, Brian Willen 28, Richard Bakehouse 41, Augustine Fell 33, Thomas Brigge 30, Thomas Person 25, and John Cowper 25. All eight wished to continue in the religious life: at Cartmel if possible, but in another house if Cartmel were to be closed.

In addition to the religious there were thirty-seven servants, some employed within the house and others in outdoor capacities. There were ten waiting servants, nineteen officers of the household or the estate, and eight 'servants of husbandry' or farm workers, sometimes referred to as *'hinds'*. In addition there was a *'Conductor of the King's people over Cartmel Sands,'* who received £6 per year. The 'Cartership of Kent Sands'

carried a tenement at Kent's Bank and certain lands and wages. There was also an office of groom porter filled by a man named Edward Barborne who was not wanted by the canons but had been forced upon them by outside officialdom. Since Barborne is referred to as a *'King's Sergeant'* and the question of his employment at the priory was settled as late as February 1536, it appears that the crown officers, probably Legh and Layton, had inserted their own man to keep an eye on events and report back to them. The ten waiters received annual wages ranging from 6s. 8d. to 20s. This seems very little but we can suppose that they also received board and lodging. Hinds received 8s. to 16s. The officers of the priory were: brewer, baker, barber, cook, scullion, butler of the fratry, two wood-leaders, keeper of the woods, two millers, fisher, wright, pulter, fosterman, maltmaker, two shepherds and a hunter. Highest paid was the wright, while the butler of the fratry, or dining room, received the lowest wage. The annual total paid in wages for 1535 was £25 14s. The employing of a hunter is of considerable interest. Though he helped organise the hunting of deer and other game for the prior and his guests, a highly important part of his work was the killing of wolves. Estates in the north of England, with considerable numbers of calves and lambs, suffered the depredations of wolves, and the prior of Cartmel, like the abbots of Furness, Whalley, and Wyresdale, will have seen it as vital to keep down their numbers.

Despite the artificial raising by the commissioners of the annual income for 1535, Cartmel priory was closed, and the canons dispersed, in the autumn of 1536, but the Cartmel story was not finished. In the north of England the closing of religious houses had brought to a head a number of grievances that had been growing among people of various classes. This discontent quickly grew to outright insurrection, particularly in Lincolnshire, Yorkshire and then Lancashire and Westmorland: areas where the people felt that their voices, a long way from the centre of government, were not being listened to. They were deeply troubled at the closing of the monasteries and their revolt had decidedly religious overtones, which led the participants to call their movement, 'The Pilgrimage of Grace.'

By the time this movement had reached Lancashire the priory of Cartmel was closed and silent, but a curious set of circumstances brought it back to life for a short while. The Pilgrimage of Grace was the most serious threat to the stability of the realm during the reign of Henry VIII, and for a time it seemed that the insurgents were going to have their demands met. Pardons were promised for leaders and others, and the dispersal of armed bands was urged by royal officials with an undertaking that no action would be taken against them. On 12 December 1536, John Dakyn, vicar-general of the archdeaconry of Richmond, wrote to the prior of Cartmel, Richard Preston, who had already surrendered the priory, saying that all monks and canons, by the king's consent, were to return to their monasteries and resume the religious life. Prior Preston was mistrustful of such a message and instead of returning to Cartmel, he went to Preston and placed himself under royal protection in the person of the earl of Derby. The Cartmel canons, however, took Dakyn at his word and returned to the priory in the clear expectation of a fresh start.

It is unclear as to where archdeacon Dakyn had heard the message that he so eagerly promulgated, but its content was denied by officials of every kind, and through his silence, and

66

failure to confirm it, by the king himself. A general pardon for monastic rebels was issued on 22 December 1536 and it seemed that all might be well, but this was not to be. Thomas Holcroft, body servant to the king, and a man who made a fortune by obtaining the lands and property of many of the defunct monasteries in the north-west of England, had secured the legal right to the crops of Cartmel Priory produced that year and lately stored in the barns. This right had not been rescinded, and the returned canons faced the prospect of a lean winter without the corn and other supplies they would normally have had. Holcroft was as unpopular as he was uncompromising. His men turned up to seize the stored crops, and a serious altercation broke out, with local men defending the canon's claim to the stores they needed for the winter. Holcroft's men quickly dispersed the locals and, because resistance to a royal lessee was deemed to be treason, six canons and sixteen local men were taken prisoner and removed to Lancaster for investigation and possibly trial. Two of the canons and a number of the laymen had managed to escape, but the others faced a situation that, in the tense atmosphere prevailing throughout the north, was one of extreme peril. Two of the canons, Brian Willan and Thomas Briggs, were found 'not guilty' and acquitted. The other four, William Pannell, Augustine Fell, Richard Backhouse, and John Cowper, were found guilty of treason and publicly executed in Lancaster. Accompanying then to the gallows, for their part in the affray at Cartmel, were ten of the sixteen local men. They were: Peter Barwyck, Matthew Bateman, Robert Dawson, James Carter, John Blackhed, John Bigland, John Brockbank, William Crossefield, William Byrkhead and Gilbert Preston. The final closure of Cartmel Priory was one of the bloodiest and most bitter events of that unhappy period.

There is nothing left today of the claustral buildings and perimeter wall. Cloister, dormitory, refectory are gone, and all that remains is the beautiful gatehouse, built c.1340, that stands now in the street at some distance from the church, and is, to the casual observer, unrelated to it. This building has been put to many uses since the Dissolution. From 1624 to 1791 it was a school, and its manorial courtroom has also served as both Methodist chapel and billiard-room. The priory church at Cartmel remains: a splendid monument as well as a thriving parish church. The first point noted by the visitor is its size and elegance, its tower topped by a great lantern set diagonally, its interior resembling in no small way that of an English cathedral. This was a monastery church for only eight or nine canons, and it might be asked why they needed a church so large. The reason, partly at least, is that this was the church used by the faithful of the area, and it survived because it was their only place of worship. Cartmel church has undergone various changes over the centuries, but it stands as a proud reminder of what was once a thriving monastic community that served the local population for almost 350 years.

Destruction of the priory buildings and perimeter wall left the gate lodge at Cartmel in an isolated position so that the town grew around it

BURSCOUGH PRIORY,
DEDICATED TO ST. NICHOLAS

Burscough priory, a house of Augustinian canons, was founded c.1190 by Robert Fitz Henry, lord of Lathom and Knowsley, who made a modest endowment of land for its support. This comprised half the manor of Burscough, including the vill of Martin, and the vill of Ormskirk. The vill of Dalton, near Wigan, was given in the thirteenth century by Robert de Lathom, and numerous small parcels of land, with a large number of rents, were given by local landholding families. For example, the vill of Ridgate, in Prescot parish was given in 1283 by Henry de Lathom, lord of the manor of Tarbock. There was also land at Ellel, Lancaster. These endowments amounted in total to little more than 3,500 acres, much of it poor quality. The land around Ormskirk and Burscough incorporated a great deal of 'moss', or peat bog, and also contained the extensive Martin Mere. At the end of its life Burscough could produce a net income of only £80 7s. 6d., of which as little as £7 7s. 6d. actually came from its land. The priory was indeed fortunate to have in its initial endowment the local church of Ormskirk, the parish church of Huyton, and the church of Flixton, Manchester, together with the chapel of St. Leonard in Knowsley. For much of its existence, Burscough Priory appointed one of its own canons vicar of Ormskirk, an arrangement that kept parochial affairs closely in the hands of the prior, and saved the stipend of a secular priest if such were to be appointed to the church.

A windfall of considerable importance came to the priory in 1381 when Alexander Neville, archbishop of York, allowed the appropriation to Burscough of the church of Radcliffe on Soar in Nottinghamshire, donated by John de Winwick, in order to create some revenue that might help to relieve the poverty of the priory caused by the 'pestilence.' This referred to the Black Death which had come to Lancashire in 1349 with a mortality rate that was very high: perhaps as much as half the population in some parts of the county. Nor was the mid-century visitation the only one. There were periodic outbreaks for the next hundred years or so, and recovery was seriously retarded because of the constant attrition of the young people whose labour was needed for the rebuilding of the economy, and whose breeding potential was vital to the re-growth of the population. Indeed, it was probably an outbreak of the plague some 55 years before the Black Death that led to the empowering of the prior of Burscough by Pope Boniface VIII, (1294-1303,) to ordain six of the canons early, providing they were over the age of twenty. There are plenty of examples of this concession to make up shortages in clergy numbers caused by epidemics.

In 1286, the prior and convent of Burscough had rights of a borough bestowed on Ormskirk, and obtained a market and a five days fair in the town. These privileges were confirmed by Edward II in 1323 when he was visiting Upholland. As holder of market rights, the prior imposed fines for breaches of the assize of bread and ale, a claim that led to dispute with the officers of Henry, earl of Lancaster, whose right this had formerly been. In 1339, Henry conceded the claim to the prior of Burscough in return for the annual payment of 6s. 8d. (Half a mark).

Prior Thomas Litherland, a man who held office for a very long time: from 1347 or earlier, to his resignation in 1385, found himself in trouble with the civil law. In 1347 a Lancashire knight, Sir John de Dalton, assisted by a number of Lancashire men, forcibly abducted a young widow named Marjery de la Beche from her home, the manor of Beams in Wiltshire. Blood was shed, with two men killed and others injured. This was a considerable

70

affront to the crown since, although King Edward III and his eldest son, *'the Black Prince'*, were away fighting the French, the king's third son, Lionel, duke of Clarence, governing the realm for his father, was staying in the manor house while the violent Lancastrians cut and thrust all about them in support of Dalton's abduction of the widow. Dalton brought the young woman to Lancashire where he took refuge at Upholland from his pursuers. Prior Litherland of Burscough was said to have been implicated in this affair, whether as one of the violent men in Wiltshire, he would have been young at the time, or as one who colluded in Dalton's escape and hiding, is uncertain. All was quickly cleared up, however. Dalton, a soldier of renown, was well known to the king, having fought alongside him at the Battle of Crecy, (1346) and was clearly held high in royal regard. Edward III pardoned him, *'on account of his good service'*, and no further action was taken against anyone, including prior Litherland.

The story does not end there, however. Sir John Dalton and Margery de la Beche were married in 1348, an outcome that suggests we are looking at an elopement rather than an abduction. There was no happy ending. Margery died in 1349, perhaps in childbirth, a very common cause of death among young women, or quite probably of the Black Death, which, as we saw above, struck Lancashire that year. Sir John lived for another twenty years; a man of violence and warfare, he met a violent end in 1369 at the hands of William Garstang. We do not know the circumstances, but it would seem that Garstang was acting in self-defence since he received a full pardon from the king shortly afterwards. Prior Litherland, whatever his role in this affair, stayed on at the priory until his resignation, presumably on grounds of age, in 1385.

Records of monastic houses contain snippets of information that are tantalisingly vague. For example, in 1386, Pope Urban VI, (1378-89,) made reference to certain un-named *'sons of iniquity'* who were detaining and concealing the land and goods of the priory. He ordered the abbot of Chester to require restitution of the priory's property on pain of excommunication for the guilty ones. What the wrongdoers had actually done, is not at all clear, but this was not long after the Peasants' Revolt of 1381, and the authority of Richard II was being called into question. It was a time when landowners, including monastic ones, were held in considerable contempt by the lower classes, and it may be that here we have an example of men who were nominally unfree, withholding rents and labour services owed to their lord, the prior of Burscough.

The pope, far away in Rome, commonly concerned himself with the affairs of monasteries large and small throughout Christendom. An example of this is the order of Pope Boniface IX (1389-1404) which declared a four year relaxation of penance and four quadragenes to penitents who visited the priory on St. Nicholas' day and gave alms for the conservation of Burscough priory and church.

It is inevitable that in considering the very long life of the English monasteries, and the large numbers of men, and women, associated with them over three or four centuries, that we will come across some who were tainted with wrongdoing of one kind or another. Though we might suppose a fairly blameless career for most of those who entered the contemplative life, indeed, that is what was expected of them and was therefore not remarkable, we have clear evidence of a few who, either from lust, cupidity, or a simple propensity for breaking the rules, have found their way into the records, not for their piety but for their sins. For example, in 1454, charges of divination, sortilege, and the black art were brought against the prior, Robert Woodward, canon Robert Fairwise, and William Bolton, vicar of Ormskirk. On investigation of these charges, the diocesan bishop of Coventry and Lichfield found that a man named Robert, a necromancer, had declared that he could reveal to them a hidden treasure, having first been paid the sum of £10. What followed appears almost comical to the twenty-first century mind, but in the fifteenth it was a matter to which many gave credence. After swearing secrecy on the blessed-sacrament, they handed it in a '*pyx*' to Robert. Three circles with triangles were drawn on the ground, in each of which stood one of the priests, the vicar of Ormskirk with the host suspended on his breast, and a rod, probably a divining rod, in his hand. The only gain in this affair seems to have been Robert's £10, since no treasure was evidently forthcoming. The bishop, despite protestations from the three that they had not invoked demons, or made any sacrifice to them, suspended them all from priestly office for two years and from receiving the sacraments, unless on their death bed. William Bolton was removed from the vicarage of Ormskirk and the prior was obliged to resign. Though the bishop lifted their suspensions after a few months, none was restored to any office. The former prior was granted a pension of ten marks, together with a suitable chamber in the priory and the rations in meat, bread and beer of two canons.

Almost fifty years later, in 1511, there was another scandal at the priory, though again we are not told the details. Whatever it was, it was serious enough for the diocesan bishop to order the removal from office of the prior, John Barton. This highlights a problem encountered by small priories when a new prior was needed. The bishop was of the view that none of the canons at Burscough was suitable for the post of prior, and so he replaced Barton with Robert Harvey, a canon of Kenilworth Priory, Warwickshire.

After some 350 years, when officers were visiting and assessing the monasteries at the behest of Henry VIII with a view to closing them down and seizing their assets, Burscough stood little chance of survival. Though its stated income in 1535 was only £80 7s. 6d., and the commissioners in the following year raised the figure to £122 5s. 7d., it was marked down for immediate closure. There were only five canons in residence, all ordained priests, one of whom had been declared by royal commissioners, Layton and Legh, inevitably perhaps, to have been guilty of sexual incontinence, and only one stating a desire to remain a canon of the order. The team of commissioners that had visited Upholland also came to Burscough. They were: Sir William Leyland, Sir Richard Assheton, Sir Thomas Halsall, Thomas Burgoyne, auditor; Thomas Armer, receiver. The commissioners found the priory church and buildings to be in good condition, and the earl of Derby was anxious to save the church if possible since many members of his family were buried there. He proposed to install a secular priest at his own expense who while conducting divine service there for the souls of his ancestors would also provide for the spiritual needs of those who lived in the area. Derby's plans came to nothing; the church and buildings were duly demolished, despite his urging delay because of the uncertainty caused by the Pilgrimage of Grace.

Burscough Priory was a significant provider of employment. There were twenty-two waiting servants and household officers and eighteen farm servants, or 'hinds of husbandry.' Nor was charity neglected by the canons, though their means were limited. At the closure there were two people receiving board for life, and a leper hospital was maintained at the priory. There was also an annual disbursement of £7 to charity.

The priory buildings, together with lead and bells, were valued at £148 10s.and the moveable goods at £230 3s. 4d. The church ornaments were assessed at £97, plate and jewellery £27, chattels of all sorts, £37, household linen and implements, £31,

74

stock of corn, £35. The house, and its 350 years of history, like so many others of its kind, was quickly erased from the landscape, and from the society of which it had been for so long an integral part. The site and lands were granted in 1547, to Sir William Paget, a leading adviser to the king.

Very little remains to be seen of Burscough Priory and the site does not normally attract visitors. In fact, all that remains are two piers belonging to the 175-foot church. These are of high quality and suggest a very handsome building. They are best seen from trains passing on the railway from Preston to Liverpool.

All that remains of the 175-foot church at Burscough Priory
are two elegant piers

COCKERHAM PRIORY,
DEDICATED TO SAINT MICHAEL

The Augustinian priory of Cockerham is one of the smallest, and least well-known, of Lancashire's medieval monasteries. Its origin is bound up with that of its much larger neighbour, Cockersand Abbey, and we may reasonably conclude that if Cockersand had not been built, then there would have been no priory at Cockerham. Cockersand Abbey occupies a site that stood originally within the manor of Cockerham, and there was, around the end of the twelfth century, a decade or more of legal disputation as to whether Cockersand, a house of Premonstratensian canons, had any right to be there within a manor belonging to the Augustinian house of St. Mary of the Meadow, Leicester. (This matter is discussed in the chapter on Cockersand Abbey).

The manor of Cockerham stands on the boundary between the hundreds of Lonsdale and Amounderness. At the time of Domesday Book, the western part of the manor, known as Crimbles, lay within Amounderness, the remainder being part of Lonsdale. In the twelfth century it was part of the lordship of William of Lancaster I, baron of Kendale and lord of Wyresdale, who c.1153 gave the whole manor, together with its church of St. Michael, and dependent chapel of Ellel, to Leicester Abbey. The gift of a manor to a distant monastery was not unusual in medieval England. Barons and religious figures had contact through family, and friends in distant parts of the land. This was a comprehensive endowment, most of the customary rights, privileges and responsibilities of a manor being transferred to the abbey. There was a windmill and a watermill, producing a steady income for the holder of the manor, locals being obliged to grind their corn in them. The canons of Leicester held at Cockerham: view of frankpledge, free warren, a manorial court convened at three-weekly intervals, mortuary rights, heriots and wreck of the sea, from all of which they stood to profit.

Once the abbey of Cockersand was established the abbot of Leicester became concerned lest there should be encroachment onto his Cockerham possession and its various legal rights and privileges. He therefore dispatched, c.1207, a number of his Augustinian canons from Leicester to set up a small priory or cell at Cockerham and safeguard his interests there against the Premonstratensians at Cockersand, of whom he was so suspicious. The initial group consisted of three canons, one to be in charge and, possibly, styled prior. The parish church of Cockerham was at that stage being served by a secular priest, an appointee of Leicester Abbey, and he was to remain in post for life, after which the number of canons was to be increased to four.

The status of the monastery at Cockerham remained strictly that of a cell; it was never independent, and its prior and canons remained subject to recall by the abbot of Leicester. This small group of two, three, and sometimes four, canons served the parish as vicar and curates, while running the manor and guarding the interests of their mother-house. No conventual buildings were constructed, the canons living in, '*a hall with chambers over*', together with garden and dovecote, enjoying a level

77

of domestic comfort not shared by their brethren at Leicester, and most certainly not by their Cockersand neighbours on the bleak shore little more than a mile distant.

Cockerham is one of the larger manors in south Lonsdale, covering 5,809 acres. Its land was of mixed character in the middle ages. There was peat bog, or moss, extensive salt marsh, and a fair amount of good arable land and pasture. The canons lived off the produce of the manor, sending back to Leicester profits from rents and sales, particularly of wool. Their diet was as good as that of any in the district, with beef, mutton, pork, poultry and wildfowl readily available, along with peas, beans and garden vegetables such as brassicas. Much of their bread would have been made from oats, though they would have been able to bring in wheat from time to time, probably from the East Midlands estates of their mother-house. They also supplemented their diet with fish, both from the sea and from their domestic fishpond, which may still be seen in the pasture above the church.

Cockerham, like almost all the other manors in north Lancashire, was favoured by good pasture. The plentiful rainfall of the area makes for excellent grass, which has been exploited from earliest times as pasture and as hay. This has meant that cheese has long been an important source of protein in the diet, and accounts for the growth of the Lancashire cheese industry. Cockerham is doubly favoured with pasture. The higher parts of the manor, the fields around the church for example, have provided high quality grazing for many centuries. The sportsfield behind the village-hall clearly shows ridge and furrow ploughmarks dating from a time when it was cultivated as part of the common-field strip-system. Such ploughing had ceased by 1500 as the pastoral economy was extended, and men began to count their wealth not in cash but in cattle. The other aspect of pasture that Cockerham possesses, and few other manors do, is the salt marsh. Tides come and go over the imperceptibly sloping shore and produce there a sea-washed turf that has been used as sheep-pasture since time immemorial. The flocks retreat before the incoming tide, and then, as it ebbs, they follow it out again, always sure of rich grass. Cockerham wool, reared on this tidal pasture, appears in the financial records of Leicester Abbey. The gift of the manor of Cockerham to Leicester Abbey was further enhanced by the valuable additional donation by William of Lancaster of common of pasture in all of his lands within Lonsdale and Amounderness.

Manor and church were simply regarded as a taxable unit, regardless of the presence of the Augustinian canons. In 1292 it was assessed for £13 in tax, though this figure was reduced to £3 6s. 8d. after Cockerham had been devastated that year by the Scots. Like other manors, it suffered badly from the Black Death of 1349-50 when income from tithes was reduced by half.

Towards the end of the thirteenth century the abbot of Leicester embarked on a policy of running down the involvement of his canons on the Cockerham estate. Around 1286 he installed a stipendiary vicar, and then made the appointment a perpetual one. Most of the canons were withdrawn at this time, though there was still a presence. One canon remained to act as warden, and was referred to as *custos* or *gardianus*. This points to a system of renting out the lands of the estate instead of cultivating them as part of the abbey's own agricultural enterprise. We have a fifteenth-century document that clearly shows the division of the manor of Cockerham into substantial holdings for which rent was paid to the warden, for Leicester Abbey. First mentioned is the demesne land of the canons themselves, comprising 63 acres of arable and 58 of meadow with a watermill and a windmill. Then comes a list of holdings in the hands of substantial farmers, as many of them remain today. These are: Bankhouse, Thursland (with saltpits), Hillam, Marshes, Little Crimbles, Great Crimbles with Harestones, Wrampool, Hardhead, Laithwaite, Damhead, Crookay, Sinthwaite, Brileshed, Ranstey, Brookshed and Upton. There were also twenty-nine saltpits paying £8 11s. 8d., while further rents were payable from properties in Ashton, Kirkland, Thurnham , Ellel, Holleth and Cockersand. There was entitlement to payment of *'fold halfpennies'* and *'cawce halfpennies'*, two examples of the numerous taxes, dues and exactments levied upon medieval country folk. The former relates to the penning, or folding, of sheep, while the latter concerns *'urban pavage:'* the maintenance of footpaths in the town or village. In this particular case the paths are more likely to have been through the fields and moss.

This arrangement remained in place for the greater part of 200 years, coming to an end in 1477 when the last canon was withdrawn and the whole manor of Cockerham was let to John Calvert for the annual sum of £83 6s. 8d.. A condition of his lease stated that Calvert must provide board and lodgings for one or two canons and their horses for a week, when they came from Leicester on periodic visits of inspection.

Fishpond apart, there is nothing now visible to indicate the presence of this small monastic community. The canons' residence and other buildings have vanished and their location is unclear, though Cockerham Hall Farm is a possible site. It is likely that this

80

was indeed the site, since throughout Lancashire we find farm houses referred to as halls because they were formerly the residence of families holding manorial rights and land. Where a number of farms within a single manor are referred to as halls it is usually because the manorial land and rights were divided at some point. The church stands prominently in its original position but it is not the building known to the canons. What we now see is the reconstruction carried out in the nineteenth-century by the Lancaster architects Paley and Austin.

Leicester Abbey, Cockerham Priory's mother-house, was suppressed in 1538. It was one of the largest houses in the order with around forty canons in its early days, and was the third richest Augustinian house in England after Cirencester, Gloucestershire, and Merton, Surrey. The abbey's possessions, including the manor and church of Cockerham, passed to the crown. It remained in the tenancy of the Calvert family for many years after the Dissolution of the Monasteries. In 1560 it was let to Thomas Calvert by Queen Elizabeth for 90 years at a rent of £51 6s. The manor was evidently purchased from the crown in 1602 by John Calvert, son and heir of Thomas, and more than a century later it was still in the hands of members of the family.

FURNESS ABBEY,
DEDICATED TO SAINT MARY

Furness Abbey was by far the largest and richest of the Lancashire monasteries. Among the Cistercian houses of England only Fountains Abbey was richer. This is not to say that these houses were at the top of the financial scale. Many of the old Benedictine abbeys had incomes much greater than either Furness or Fountains.

At its foundation in July 1124, this community of monks was not at Furness, nor was it Cistercian. The founder, Stephen of Blois, later King Stephen, established a house of Savignac monks at Tulketh, Preston, where it remained until 1127 when he removed it to Bekanesgill, a remote site in the Furness peninsula. The reason for the move is not clear, but the Savignacs quickly settled at Furness and built one of the finest monasteries in the North of England. Twenty years later, the Furness monks, like all the others of their order, became Cistercian.

Sturdy Norman arches at Furness Abbey

Furness Abbey claimed pre-eminence among English Cistercian houses because of its foundation date at Tulketh in 1124. The next senior house was Waverley Abbey in Surrey, founded in 1128. The foundation of the Tulketh site and the removal to Furness in 1127 both pre-date Waverley's foundation, but precedence was eventually given to Waverley since it was founded as a Cistercian house, while Furness was still a Savignac house that did not become Cistercian until 1147.

As a house of the esteemed Cistercian order, and with a royal founder, Furness attracted extensive benefactions. Its new territory included the whole of Furness, and the manor of Ulverston along with its founder's valuable fishery in the Lune at Lancaster, and as the foundation of a man soon to be king, it grew rapidly and continued to grow under Stephen's successors down to Henry IV. Its widespread estates, rights and privileges were to be found in the northern counties, but its location made it vulnerable to Scottish raiders and its coastal position to Irish incursion. This was not a house noted for its scholars, chroniclers or statesmen, rather, it was a great feudal estate in the northern marches of England that had dealings with the Scottish kingdom and its barons, and established itself as an extensive agricultural, stock-rearing and industrial enterprise.

One of the strangest characters in the history of Furness was a young man called 'Wimund' who entered the abbey towards the middle of the twelfth-century. Though of humble origin he had exceptional ability and was chosen to lead a group from the abbey being sent to manage affairs in the Isle of Man. The islanders recognised his abilities and requested that he become their bishop, which he duly did. He soon became accustomed to the exercise of authority and threw aside his episcopal duties to gather a body of men and a fleet with which to raid and plunder the north-west of England and the west coast of Scotland. He passed from novice to monk, to bishop and finally to robber baron. Eventually he was captured by the people he had terrorised, blinded and mutilated and sent to end his days, defiant to the end, at Byland Abbey.

In 1535 Furness Abbey was said to have an annual net income in excess of £805: a substantial figure. This was due to the size and diversity of its enterprises. As a monastery in the hills and moors of northern England it was mainly concerned with stock rearing and agriculture. Figures from the late thirteenth-century will give some idea of the extent to which Furness was involved in the large-scale production, not only of wool, but of arable crops. In 1297 the abbey was said to have forty-four carucates in demesne. If we allow 120 acres per carucate, this amounts to 5,280 acres of land in concentrated, regular use, much in permanent pasture, some under cultivation. At their granges in Lancashire, Cumberland and Yorkshire the monks of Furness had 5,000 sheep in total, worth £300 and yielding £100 per annum in wool sales, namely twenty sacks of wool at 100 shillings per sack. There were also 200 lambs at 5 shillings apiece. This is an unusually small number of lambs from a total of 5,000 sheep, most of which would have been ewes of breeding age, and we must presume that the figures for 1297 were compiled early in the lambing season, when many lambs had yet to be born, or later in the year when most had been disposed of.

Superb fonts in the Early English style

The production and sale of wool was a major industry for the monastic houses, particularly Cistercian, in the north of England. The monks are often credited with the introduction and development of improved strains of sheep and superior wool, from sheep reared on marginal land that was otherwise of little use. Recent scholarship, however, tends not to support such a view. Rather, some argue, the monks, when they moved onto previously unused land, introduced established agricultural and administrative methods, not revolutionary ones. Though many Cistercian houses in the north of England clearly did have large flocks – Holmcultram, Fountains, Rievaulx and Newminster, for example, all had some 10,000 sheep at the end of the thirteenth-century – monastic wool output represented a very small proportion of the national total. Most of England's wool at this time was sold to wool-merchants from Florence and other cities of northern Italy. Some of their records have survived, notably those of a merchant called Francesco Pegolotti, which suggest that in 1273, as little as 3-4% of wool exported from England may have come from monastic sources. Furthermore, much of the monastic wool was of a quality that did not indicate the kind of improvement in sheep so often attributed to Cistercian breeders, Wool from upland pastures such as those belonging to Furness, was of very poor quality and fetched the lowest prices in the country. Nonetheless, ownership of extensive pasture and the raising of large numbers of sheep placed many of the northern religious houses in a strong financial position. So valuable was wool in the medieval economy, that houses such as Furness were able to raise capital by selling their '*clip*' several years in advance.

On their demesne estates in Lancashire and Cumberland, the abbey owned 482 draft oxen, worth a total of £149 10s. in 1297. This is a huge number of oxen, representing 60 plough teams at eight beasts per team. At roughly 5s. 10d. per ox we can readily see the level of capital owned by the abbey. Cultivation was carried out almost entirely by ox-drawn ploughs but an ordinary villein could not normally aspire to ownership of a plough and team. He may have part-owned it, collectively with a group of neighbours, or simply relied on the ploughing of strips in the common fields with teams owned by the manor of which he was an unfree tenant, in this case, Furness Abbey. When we consider the 60 teams owned by the abbey it highlights the sheer scale of its landholdings, and also the widespread distribution of its estates, particularly since there were 96 further oxen kept at Winterburn near Skipton.

There was a point in the middle ages when the ox, the agricultural unit of power, began to give way to the horse. It was accepted that the horse was superior to the ox by a ratio of around two to one, and in many parts of Europe it had virtually superseded the ox in agriculture by the end of the twelfth-century. On the Elton estate of Ramsey Abbey, Huntingdonshire, we find in 1125 some forty oxen and only two horses. Forty years later, however, the number of oxen has fallen to twenty-four and the horses increased to eight. Such was not the case in the backward north of England where horses, even at the end of the thirteenth-century were much less common than oxen. On the abbey's estates in Lancashire and Cumberland in 1297, there were thirty mares, each worth 10 shillings, and twenty-four foals aged from two to three years at five shillings each. We are not told the type or purpose of these horses, and there were forty further mares listed on the Newby estate near Ingleton. This is a large number and, since they were presumably not being used for agricultural work, they were evidently being bred as saddle horses, or '*palfreys*,' for sale on the open market. At ten shillings apiece this would bring in a handsome profit. There was a major debate in the thirteenth-

86

century on the relative merits of ox and horse and the agricultural authority of the day, Walter of Henley, declared himself firmly in favour of the ox, largely on the grounds of maintenance costs. It may be that the Furness monks continued to use the ox because it was cheaper to feed, though perhaps they found it more efficient in the heavy clay soil.

Cattle were, of course, a major part of the abbey's economy. On its various holdings in Lancashire and Cumberland there were 186 cows valued at £46 10s. in total, while at the grange of Winterburn, there were 80 more cows, and 130 at Ingleton. Most of these animals were milk cows supplying a major cheese industry; it was also common for sheep milk to be used for this purpose. We can see that a large quantity of cheese was produced by Furness Abbey on its various estates. If we take the 130 cows at Ingleton, and assume roughly 210 pounds of cheese per cow, per year, we find something approaching 28,000 pounds of cheese from that estate, a figure greatly increased if ewes' milk is included. Much of the abbey's cheese output found its way onto the market in towns and boroughs such as Skipton, Ulverston and Lancaster where four pounds of cheese cost one penny.

With cows producing a calf roughly each year, and 50% of the calves being male, an inevitable by-product of this intensive dairy farming was the ox. The fate of the male calf was fairly stark. It might be slaughtered early and eaten as veal, or castrated, either to be reared as a bullock for beef, or allowed to develop as an ox for heavy work; only a select few were retained as stud bulls.

Much of the abbey's agricultural activity took place on distant manors run as granges. Some were several days' travel from the central authority of the abbot, which placed great responsibility on those appointed to run them. In the order's early days the men recruited to perform this duty were '*conversi*,' lay-brothers, who, though sworn members of the Cistercian order, were required to take little part in the complex liturgical life of the monastery so that they might concentrate on whatever secular task they had been given by the abbot. Such men were recruited for their skills: masons, carpenters, brewers and others worked around the monastery itself, but the main group of lay-brothers was made up of farm workers, skilled in stock and estate management before joining the abbey, and were sent out by the abbot to run estates, or granges, often at a great distance.

A prosperous grange of Furness Abbey was that of Stalmine, situated on the River Wyre. There the abbey held 562 acres, mainly of good agricultural land, although it did include some moss. This estate was a long way from Furness by the tedious land route, but a relatively short journey by sea: directly across Morecambe Bay and into the River Wyre where Stalmine lies a short distance up-river on the tidal reach. There would have been regular inspections of the grange by the abbot and his senior brethren, and also regular shipment of produce from Stalmine to the abbey. We do not normally know the names of the lay-brothers in granges up and down the country, but at Stalmine we have two names that are probably of men holding the post of *grangarius*, or granger. The first of these was a man called Hamo, son of Henry de Stainall, a township adjacent to Stalmine. Henry was a local man of some standing whose son would have been born within a few hundred yards of Stalmine Grange. At a date before 1235, Hamo

88

entered the community of Furness as a lay-brother, and though we know nothing of his subsequent career, it is distinctly possible that he was taken on by the abbot specifically to work at the grange. He would have had a close knowledge of people and conditions there and, coming from a good local family, would have been ideal, first as assistant, and then grangarius. Almost a century later we find a man who was fairly certainly grangarius at Stalmine. He was Roger de Wyral, lay-brother, who appeared in court around 1310, and again in 1311, together with the Abbot of Furness, in a case dealing with common of pasture in Stalmine. Grass: that most valuable of Lancashire crops, was the subject of endless litigation. As long as an abbey was running its own agricultural enterprise, the lay-brothers were valuable men, but the exigencies of the economic climate led landowners, lay and monastic, towards a system under which they rented out their estates, rather than farmed them for themselves. This, among other factors, led to the decline and virtual disappearance of the lay-brother.

Beaumont at Lancaster was one of the most important of the Furness granges, as was that of Hawkshead. The building at Hawkshead may still be seen: a splendid example of a Cistercian grange from which not only was the agricultural enterprise conducted, but the manor of Hawkshead was run in feudal style. Courts were held, disputes decided, and malefactors hanged, all in the name of the abbot. Feudal justice at this level was commonly administered by great abbeys such as Furness. Their abbots were men of baronial status, who often held *infangenthef* and *outfangenthef*: the right to administer capital punishment within their bailiwick. The abbey also maintained a gallows at Dalton.

Hawkshead Grange: property of Furness Abbey; it is a fine example of a
monastic grange and of vernacular architecture

The granges of Furness were numerous, inevitably so
given the widespread distribution of the abbey's estates. In
addition to those already noted at Stalmine, Beaumont and
Hawkshead, the rental at the abbey's closure in 1537 shows
numerous others, supervised at that date, not by lay-brothers but
by bailiffs who kept an eye on the tenants and collected rents on
behalf of the abbot. There were major estates in Yorkshire, and
many in the Lake District, fairly close to the abbey, but just too far
away to be supervised directly from the house itself. These
included: Coniston, Waterhead, Brathay, Skelwith, Sawrey, and
Grisedale.

It was not only agriculture and stock rearing that brought
such a high level of prosperity to Furness Abbey. The Furness
peninsula contains extensive deposits of ore, from which good
quality iron was produced. Some of this was used for the abbey's
own ploughshares, chains, harness fittings, nails, bolts, and a
thousand other items made in forges, overseen in the twelfth and

thirteenth centuries no doubt, by sturdy lay-brothers recruited as blacksmiths. In Furness alone the woods supplied fuel for three forges and the streams powered five water mills. There was a great surplus of iron that could be sold on the open market, as pig iron rather than ore, along with cheese, wool, hides and other produce of the estates in the peninsula and beyond. To carry these goods to distant markets would have been virtually impossible by land, and so the abbey was inevitably drawn into the shipping business. Seagoing vessels were maintained for the transportation of the abbey's produce, for bringing in necessities, for maintaining relations with powerful men in Ireland, Man and Scotland, and for general commercial use in the Irish Sea.

For an abbey of such a size, Furness held few churches. A Benedictine or Cluniac house of similar size might have held twelve or fifteen churches and chapels from which it drew income. The Cistercians, however, were reluctant in their early days to have anything to do with matters outside their own houses and lands. They did relax this stricture but as a result of it we find major houses such as Furness with fewer churches than we might find belonging to some houses of other orders less than half its size. There were three appropriated churches of Furness Abbey: Millom, Urswick and Dalton. There was also an altar in the church of Saint Michael at York.

Because of its geographical situation, Furness invariably found itself involved in political affairs concerning Scotland and the Isle of Man. In the early years of the abbey the border between England and Scotland was somewhat vaguely defined and the Furness monks looked northward as readily as they did to the south. In 1211, for example, an abbot of Furness, Nicholas of Meaux, was consecrated at Melrose Abbey. The westerly position of the abbey also placed it within an Irish sphere; the bishop who consecrated Nicholas was the bishop of Down. Affinity with Scotland did not last, however. In 1316 the whole of the Furness district was devastated by the Scots under Robert Bruce and the abbey suffered badly. A second Scottish invasion, in 1322, brought great destruction upon Cumberland but the abbot, John of Cockerham, was instrumental in saving the abbey from despoliation by going to the Scottish camp and treating with the enemy leadership. He later entertained them at the abbey and they went away, leaving the house untouched.

Complex door in late Norman style

The end for Furness Abbey was difficult and unpleasant. By the later years of Henry VIII, some of the new nobility, and the increasingly independent and confident gentry, were beginning to exert their growing influence and to question the position of the monasteries and the land they held. Furness, which had taken little or no part in public affairs for more than a century, found it difficult to cope with powerful men who were not as supportive of religious houses as such men had once been. For example, at

Stalmine the tenants of the abbey had been accustomed to dig turf with which to make fires for salt production. This concession was on land where Furness Abbey held rights of turbary, but Nicholas Butler of Out Rawcliffe and Stalmine declared that the abbey had no such right, and arrived with armed men to put a violent and menacing stop to the turf digging. Finding themselves in a position increasingly under threat, abbots and monks resorted to the payment of subsidies to powerful men in an attempt to maintain their position. Such payments were made by Furness to the dukes of Norfolk and Suffolk, the earl of Wiltshire, to Thomas Cromwell as Master of the Rolls, and also as Royal Secretary, to the Chancellor of the Duchy of Lancaster, to Sir Thomas Wharton and, by order of the king, to Thomas Holcroft, royal body servant. Rumours of corruption were rife, and accusations of fraud and malpractice were circulated. The last abbot of Furness, Roger Pele, was particularly apprehensive of his position and attempted to make it secure by paying £200 to the crown for his admission to office, and an annual pension to Thomas Cromwell.

Abbot Roger was evidently a weak man, quite unsuited to the stress of his position in such troubled times. He lost the respect of his monks and tenants alike and the Commissioners, Layton and Legh, were particularly scathing in their criticism of him. They even installed a friar, Robert Legate, at the abbey to preach to the monks and to report back to them on the words and deeds of a monastic body now infused with the ideas surrounding the Pilgrimage of Grace, the insurrection that had taken hold in many parts of the North. The rebels wanted to redress some of their grievances over the feudal obligations that they increasingly resented, but they also felt strongly about the Oath of Supremacy. The Bishop of Rome, they asserted, was head of the church, not the King of England, and they were determined that such a position would soon be restored. This was a highly dangerous position for the monks of Furness to be taking, and with the hills and valleys around them alive with insurrection, and the monks talking treason among themselves their situation was one of great peril. Some of the monks were active in their support of the insurgents and actively recruited men on their behalf. The prior, Brian Garner, ordered the tenants of the abbey to meet the rebels in their best array, and threatened death and destruction to those who refused. By the early weeks of 1537 any confidence the monks may still have had in the abbot had evaporated, and he feared for his life so that he dared not go alone in darkness to the abbey church.

Inevitably, royal commissioners in the persons of the earls of Derby and Sussex, arrived at the abbey to assess the situation, but were met by a wall of silence. The abbot was removed from the house and taken to Whalley where he was interviewed at length by the earl of Sussex who wanted to know if abbot Roger would be willing to surrender the abbey to the crown. On 5 April he signed a document of surrender and was returned to Furness where a second document was drawn up and signed by abbot, prior and twenty-eight monks. The monks were offered the option of joining other religious houses but declared themselves unworthy to do so and were granted a pension of 40s., together with permission to quit the contemplative life. The last abbot of Furness, Roger Pele, ended his days as parson of Dalton.

Robert Southwell, acting for the crown, came to the abbey on 23 June to supervise the monks' departure, to value the abbey's possessions and to make arrangements for the future on behalf of tenants and employees. He was particularly solicitous on their behalf, arranging pensions for the beadsmen, and making a special plea on behalf of the tenants such as the *'seventy-two tall fellows who occupy Beaumont Grange'*. It is perhaps not possible to

94

enumerate the tenants and employees of Furness Abbey. In addition to hinds, herdsmen, shepherds and ploughmen, there were several lay officers of the abbey, some of whom clearly indicate by their title or function the baronial character of a large abbey such as this. These include a high steward: the abbey's representative in the outside world, and eighteen bailiffs, of whom the highest in rank was the *'bailiff of the liberty,'* namely coroner and judicial deputy to the abbot. There was also an important functionary with the title, *'master of the fells,'*

At the abbey Southwell ordered the removal and melting down of the lead from flashings and guttering, and the demolition of the church and steeple. The cattle were sold off, and traders came, even from the south of England, to buy goods and chattels, livestock and produce at this favourable market. This vast baronial, agricultural and industrial enterprise was brought to an abrupt end. In 1536 Furness Abbey was still intact. In 1537 it was gone.

Today the ruins of Furness are extensive and give a clear impression of the imposing nature of the establishment that once stood there. The sixteenth century despoilers removed roofs, timber, lead and glass which left everything open to the elements, and the process of dilapidation immediately set in. Some stone was removed also, but even after almost 400 years the size and majestic nature of the buildings can clearly be discerned. The extent and grandeur of the church, 300 feet in length, is evident, even though there are whole sections of wall completely absent. Particularly imposing are the Norman arches in the cloister, one of which is the entrance to the chapter house, the sedilia in the presbytery, and many other features such as the ceiling of the infirmary chapel.

Superb sedilia at Furness Abbey; sadly broken centuries ago

This is a highly popular site, visited today by large numbers of people, and allowing those who come to experience something of the atmosphere in which monks lived their contemplative lives, where the young were educated, the sick cared for and the elderly allowed tolive in peace and dignity. How poignant are the ruins of Furness Abbey, more so than those of any other Lancashire house. Little more now than a tourist attraction, they exemplify to perfection what England once took for granted. The destruction of such establishments, the length and breadth of the country was a grievous loss and an act of cultural vandalism on an unprecedented and irreversible scale. The great church of Furness, though brilliantly ornamented and cathedral sized, was not even in the first rank of English abbey churches. Glastonbury, Bury Saint Edmunds, Abingdon and Saint Augustine's, Canterbury, were larger and more grand, even than most medieval cathedrals, but the spiritual importance and architectural magnificence of Furness and the rest counted for nothing as they were brought crashing down in rubble and ignominy.

WHALLEY ABBEY,
DEDICATED TO SAINT MARY

The story of Whalley Abbey does not begin at Whalley, but at Stanlaw in Cheshire, a little to the east of the present Ellesmere Port. Stanlaw Abbey was a Cistercian house, founded in 1172 by John, baron of Halton, and colonised by monks from Combermere Abbey, on the Cheshire side of the county boundary, four miles from Whitchurch. Though the house at Stanlaw remained in existence for a little over 100 years: 1172-1296, it was a cheerless spot, described as "a place of comfortless desolation." It lay on mud-flats at the confluence of the Gowy and the Mersey.

The new house was given suitable lands and privileges by its founder, and attracted further donations from his descendants and from other major families of Cheshire. It also attracted much more valuable property in Lancashire after the founder's son Roger, had inherited the great feudal holdings of Pontefract and Clitheroe from his kinsman, Robert de Lacy. Roger took the de Lacy name and, as lord of the honour of Clitheroe, he and his descendants became substantial benefactors of Stanlaw Abbey and subsequently of Whalley Abbey.

Life for the monks at Stanlaw was even more austere than most Cistercians would have wished upon themselves. The buildings were subject to inundation from tidal surges that occurred in the River Mersey from time to time, until the area was reduced more or less to a swamp by a major tidal incursion in 1279. Probably because of insecure foundations, a great storm brought down the tower in 1287 and in 1289 a fire destroyed much of the abbey. After this there came further high tides which threatened, *"the total destruction of the monastery."*

A close eye had been kept on their Stanlaw foundation by the de Lacys and they eventually agreed to the transfer of the Stanlaw community to a more appropriate site. The monks represented to de Lacy that none of their estates would be suitable for a new abbey except the parish of Whalley, of which they held one fourth part. They persuaded de Lacy to grant them the church of Whalley so that they might build their new abbey on its glebe land. Their abbey of Stanlaw had been known as *Locus Benedictus*, and it was decreed that the new abbey should be known as *Locus Benedictus de Whalley*.

The north-east gate-lodge, one of Whalley Abbey's two entrances

The move to Whalley took place in 1296. There was no accommodation there for the monks and so it was necessary to arrange temporary quarters until they were able to move to their permanent site. At the time of the transfer there were thirty-five monks at Stanlaw, of whom the abbot, Robert Haworth, having resigned his abbacy, and five other monks, remained behind to run Stanlaw as a cell of the new house to be built in Lancashire. One monk went to live at the abbey's grange of Stanney, two each

98

to the granges of Marland and Staining, and another was studying at Oxford. Twenty of the monks, including their new abbot, Gregory of Norbury, took up residence in the parsonage of Whalley. This leaves three monks unaccounted for, but doubtless they were lodged in some suitable farm or rectory.

The newly arrived monks made a faltering start. There was a complaint from the nearby Cistercian abbey of Sawley that the new house was closer to it than the seven miles agreed within the order. Also the Sawley community was aggrieved because the newcomers now held the tithe of Whalley church, which they would need to feed themselves, whereas the former vicar of Whalley had been accustomed to sell his tithe corn to Sawley. Within twenty years of their arrival the monks were seeking to move again, and went so far as to obtain a site for themselves at Toxteth in Liverpool. The surrounding country at Whalley was bleak, they said, and there was a complete absence of trees to provide suitable timber for building: complaints that might surprise the visitor to Whalley today. Their request for a second move was refused, and the monks of Whalley were obliged to make the best of what they regarded as a poor choice.

The building plans envisaged sixty monks, plus a number of lay-brothers in residence. No such figure was ever reached and it is unlikely that there were many lay-brothers at any time after the arrival from Stanlaw. Though the abbey emerged as a very substantial establishment, the number of monks there seems never to have exceeded the thirty-five in residence at Stanlaw in 1296. We are fortunate in that at Whalley we can see much of the ground plan in the form of ruined walls or exposed foundations. As with all monasteries the

most impressive feature is the church. That of Whalley Abbey has entirely gone, but its foundations are there to show just how large it was. Some monasteries had large churches because part of the building was used by the general public as their place of worship. This was not normally the case with the Cistercians, particularly at Whalley where the parish church stood immediately adjacent to the abbey. The large and splendid church at Whalley was for the greater glory of God and for his worship by the monastic community. It measured 260 feet in length and was, as Owen Ashmore points out, the size of Ripon Cathedral.

Despite their dislike of the site, the monks began to come to terms with life at Whalley. The dispute with Sawley was settled amicably, even before the proposed move to Toxteth. In 1305 an agreement was made to the effect that each house was to promote the other's interests as if they were their own, and that Sawley should have first option to purchase the tithe corn from Whalley, provided they were willing to pay the current market price.

Whalley Abbey's lifetime of 240 years was marked by seemingly endless disputes of a political and financial nature. For example, the monks had obtained permission to appoint one of their own members to the vicarage of Whalley, but their bishop, Walter Langton of Lichfield, took action against them over this and achieved not only a reversal of the earlier judgement but also damages of 1,000 marks plus costs. It was not until 1310 that Langton withdrew his objections but in the meantime the abbey had paid 100 marks on account and had been obliged to sell off goods to raise the money. In 1330 bishop Northburgh of Lichfield allowed the abbot to appoint one of his own monks, followed in succession by two others, to the vicarage of Whalley. This practice became general after 1358 when Pope Innocent VI (1352-62) accepted the plea from the abbot and monks that it was inappropriate at Whalley to appoint a secular priest to a post within a monastic 'inclosure.'

Another problem arose when the abbot of Combermere, Whalley's mother-house, declared that Whalley was not paying enough to the general levy of the Cistercian order. Abbot Norbury complained that the cost of building a new abbey made it impossible to pay more. Nonetheless, the abbot of Combermere ruled that Whalley should pay as much as the two other daughter-houses, Dieulacres and Hulton, put together. Whalley was required in 1318 to pay the large sum of £212. The Whalley monks were horrified at this and went to arbitration where the figure was reduced to £80.

Though building of the new abbey was under way from the beginning, there can have been no enthusiasm for the work, given the desire of the monks to move on yet again. The final refusal of such a move, however, spurred them to take up the work in earnest. Building was a slow, deliberate process in the middle-ages, when everything was done by hand. There was also a limited building season because of the danger of freshly laid mortar freezing instead of setting, thus nullifying the mortar and rendering that stage, and every course above it, useless. Many master-builders observed a building season as short as from May to September; any risk of frost meant immediate cessation of work with mortar. The building of the great church at Whalley was thus a slow process. The foundation stone was laid in 1330 but it was not until 1380 that the first Mass was said within it. As early as 1356 there had been an accident when a stone fell from the bell-tower and killed one of the monks, Ralph of Pontefract, but we do not know how near the tower was to its full height, and there was probably still work to be done when the first Mass was said. The bells to be hung in the tower of the abbey-church were almost certainly cast at Whalley. A place as remote and inaccessible as this in the fourteenth-century could hardly have commissioned bells from some distant foundry and had them delivered. Recent archaeological work has revealed a foundry-pit containing what are fairly certainly parts of bell moulds that point to the bringing in of the bell founders to create the bells *in-situ*.

The perimeter wall was begun in 1339, the earliest gateway being that to the north-west, which still stands some 300 yards along the public road. The north-east gatehouse, which is the entrance still in use today, was only completed in its present form in 1480. Work on the claustral buildings began in the fourteenth century, the need for permanent accommodation being pressing, but building work on such structures as the hospital and the abbot's lodgings, was not completed until around 1440. Money, as much as time and the cycle of the seasons, conditioned the pace at which the work proceeded. In 1362 the monks were excused payment of the levy to the Cistercian order until they had completed the church, dormitory and refectory, and by 1366 expenditure had exceeded income by £150, leaving a debt amounting to more than £700.

Abbots of Combermere had not helped in stabilising the finances at Whalley. In 1366, Abbot Chester of Combermere conspired with a number of Whalley monks, and others, to remove Abbot Lindley from office and replace him with William Banastre. The dissidents seized the abbey, and Lindley was obliged to call for armed assistance from the sheriff and his men.

Matters settled down and the building work continued to progress towards completion, but there seem always to have been disputes and legal problems exercising the monks. There was a long-running case involving the chapel of St. Michael in Clitheroe Castle, which the monks claimed as a chapel of Whalley church, in opposition to the view of their de Lacy patron. When the chaplaincy fell vacant, de Lacy gave it to his clerk, William de Luny, an act that, according to the Whalley monks, placed his immortal soul in peril. Eventually, in 1334, a royal enquiry into the matter conceded the right of the chapel to the abbey, though the monks were required to find the sum of 300 marks for this recognition. Complicating the issue was the priest, Richard de Mosely who had been installed in the chapel by the dowager queen Isabella, only two weeks before recognition of the monks' claim had been granted by her son, Edward III. Mosely had to be compensated by a pension of £40 a year for life.

A hundred years later there were still disputes and financial problems. Some time after 1475 the rector of Slaidburn, Christopher Parsons, disputed the abbey's right to tithes of the Forest of Bowland and parts of Slaidburn.. Though these lands are at some distance from Whalley, the tithes belonged to the chapel of Clitheroe Castle and therefore to Whalley Abbey, but Parsons disputed the claim, and urged violence against abbey personnel involved in the collecting of them. In November 1480, the abbey  bursar, Christopher Thornbergh, was engaged in driving away some calves that had been paid in tithe when a mob appeared and severely beat him, urged on by Parsons with cries of, "*Kill the monk, slay the monk."* For at least fourteen years more, the rector of Slaidburn was still giving trouble to the abbey over the question of these tithes, despite royal judgements having been given against him by kings: Edward IV, Richard III and Henry VII. Finally, in 1503 a royal order was made to the effect that the Bowland men must pay their tithes to Whalley Abbey.

The original possessions of the abbey were those Cheshire lands the monks had received while still in their abbey of Stanlaw, but as their patrons assumed the name of de Lacy and acquired vast estates in Lancashire, so the abbey of Stanlaw received further benefactions in that county. The principal landholdings were the manors of: Stanney, Ashton, Acton and Willington in Cheshire; in Lancashire the monks held: Whalley, Marland, Staining, Cronton and Billington. Typical of the abbey's larger holdings in Lancashire is the manor of Staining, with its associated townships of Hardhorn and Newton, near Blackpool. This was an estate of more than 5,000 acres, much of it good land, though it did contain some moss. The large Staining estate presents a good example of the kind of complications to be found in ecclesiastical law. Staining, Hardhorn and Newton belonged to Whalley Abbey, but lay within the parish of Poulton which belonged largely to Lancaster Priory. As rector of the parish, the prior of Lancaster was entitled to receive the tithe, that is, ten per cent of produce, from the townships held by Whalley.

The tithe was a tax of ancient origin, originally designed to support the local church and its clergy. Each individual within the parish was required to contribute one tenth of crops, young beasts, and even commodities such as honey and wax. Where an individual did not raise crops or animals but made his living through trade or craft, then he must contribute one tenth of his income. Tithe was regarded as just another tax, and was as unpopular as any other. To those entitled to receive the tithe it was a great boon, and an important part of the income of a church.

104

Such a consideration lay behind the differences that existed for many years between Whalley and Lancaster. To modern eyes it certainly would seem odd that a monastery owning an estate should have to render a tenth part of its produce to another monastery.

Like most other Cistercian houses, Whalley had a number of granges through which it controlled its distant estates. In these granges some of its monks were housed during the transition between Stanlaw and Whalley. That at Staining was a major establishment, controlling a large estate with many families resident upon it. In its early days, these families were *unfree*. i.e. they were bound to the estate and required to provide certain labour services in return for the strips of land they held in the common fields. It was customary in the early days of the Cistercian order for granges to be run by *conversi*, lay-brothers of the abbey, who would have been recruited for their skills in agricultural management. Gradually, there was a shift from the running of the estate by landowners such as monasteries, to the renting out of parcels of land to individuals who were the forerunners of the tenant farmers we see today. This process had begun in the thirteenth-century, and by the late fourteenth, the Black Death having seriously reduced the working population, most abbots and other proprietors found it expedient to place their lands in the hands of tenants and rely on the rents for income. This period also saw the decline, and in many houses the disappearance, of the lay-brother, that stalwart workman in monasteries the length and breadth of the country. With lands no longer cultivated by the abbey, the lay-brother had become something of an anachronism. At Whalley in 1366 there were twenty-nine monks and one lay-brother, while at Rievaulx, one of the great Cistercian houses where, in the late twelfth century, there were 500 lay-brothers, we find in 1380, only three. During this period, the Staining estate had taken on a new appearance and documents show lists of tenants with the rents they were required to pay, and as with most monastic rents, the numbers of cocks and hens they were required to provide as part of their dues.

In addition to its estates, Whalley Abbey also had a number of churches appropriated to it. Though in its early days the Cistercian order eschewed the holding of churches, or the receiving and paying of tithes, it did not maintain this stance for long and by the time the abbey at Stanlaw was being built the Cistercian houses were falling into line with other orders and becoming landed proprietors. In addition to the parish church of Whalley, the abbey held the churches of Eccles, Rochdale and Blackburn. The income derived from these churches in 1478 was £365, while in 1521 this had risen to £592. In 1535, however, the *Valor Ecclesiasticus* gives the income from the four churches as less than half of this: a mere £272 7s. 8d. Doubtless there had been some *'constructive accounting'* employed in providing figures for this national survey. Certain fixed charges are noted in the accounts. These include the sum of £43 10s. in pensions for the vicars of the four appropriated churches. Another item of expenditure was the sum of £2 3s. 4d. as Whalley's contribution to the maintenance of St. Bernard's College at Oxford.

Benedictines, Augustinians and Cistercians set up colleges in both Oxford and Cambridge. The largest of the monastic colleges was the Cistercian St. Bernard's College, which existed

106

from 1437 to c.1542. Such was the importance placed upon learning that a Cistercian decree of 1482 required that every English house of the order with twelve monks or more must send one of them to Oxford, and if there were twenty-six or more, they must send two. John Paslew, the last abbot of Whalley, spent ten years as a student at Oxford, as did a number of others who were to become abbots. There were fees directly charged to the abbey for these student monks. It cost £9 6s. 8d. in 1521 to put a student monk through the course for the degree of Bachelor of Arts. When the monasteries were no more, their colleges also came to an end. They were not destroyed like the monasteries but absorbed into other colleges or continued under another name. St. Bernard's became St. John's College.

Whalley Abbey came to a very unhappy end. John Paslew was accused of squandering the abbey's finances on lavish new buildings, and on food and drink. Certainly, he built a new Lady Chapel, though its actual location is unclear, and largely rebuilt the abbot's lodgings. Much of the expenditure on food may possibly be accounted for by the abbey's obligation to charity and hospitality, but the exotic and costly nature of some of the items would seem to suggest indulgence on a considerable scale by the monks, or possibly a succession of guests whom the abbot was seeking to impress. In 1520 and 21, between £30 and £40 pounds was spent each year on such items as: wine, spices, figs, almonds, nutmeg, cinnamon, cloves, liquorice and sugar: hardly the fare of monks.

107

In 1535 the annual income of the abbey was stated to be over £321, which made it the second wealthiest of the Lancashire houses, though far from rich by English standards. This figure was well in excess of the £200 required to avoid closure in 1536 and had there been no further complications it would have been allowed to remain in existence, perhaps until 1539. The Pilgrimage of Grace, however, was under way, and Whalley, because of its size and position close to the Yorkshire border, was heavily influenced. Sawley Abbey, less than seven miles away, but in Yorkshire, was at the centre of the rebellion in west Yorkshire and east Lancashire, and whether or not the Whalley monks wished to avoid involvement, some of them were drawn in. In October 1536 Nicholas Tempest, a Yorkshireman prominent in the movement arrived at Whalley with 400 men at his back, and swore the abbot and monks to the cause. The arrival of Tempest and his men, and their evident welcome at the abbey placed the abbot directly in the eye of the royal officials, and inevitably, John Paslew found himself on trial for treason. He was accused of lending Tempest a horse and some plate, though Robert Aske, the acknowledged leader of the Pilgrimage of Grace, declared that he had received nothing from Whalley. On 1 January 1537 Paslew and the monks granted a pension of £6 13s. 4d. to Thomas Cromwell, probably in an attempt to gain some favour with the king's chief minister. He also wrote a letter to his fellow Cistercian abbot at Hailes Abbey in Gloucestershire, in which he declared himself to be "*sore stopped and scrased*". These were the words of an old man harassed and worried. The letter was intercepted by royal officers and Paslew was arrested, the letter presumably containing evidence against him.

The abbot, who was approaching seventy years of age, was placed on trial at Lancaster in March, convicted of treason, and hanged, drawn and quartered there. William Haydock, one of the Whalley monks, was also tried at Lancaster, but he was sent back to Whalley for execution, an event that probably gave rise to the belief that Paslew himself was executed there.

Because of the abbot's conviction for treason, the abbey and its possessions were declared forfeit to the crown, and the monks dispersed to other religious houses or to positions as secular clergy. There was vague discussion of a new beginning for the abbey, but that quickly ceased as the surrender of religious houses became general in 1538-9. In 1553 the abbey site and the manor of Whalley were sold to John Braddyl for £2,132. Braddyl was a servant of Sir Thomas Holcroft, a man we have already encountered in the process of buying up monastic property, himself a servant of Henry VIII.

The abbey at Stanlaw, and its successor at Whalley, seemed never to live up to the expectations their founder had for them. The grand design of Whalley and the expectation of 60 choir monks, plus lay-brothers, were over-ambitious. The numbers of monks declined from the original thirty-five to a mere thirteen at the end. Indeed, the great majority of people living within the walls were either servants or people kept by the charity of the abbey. At the close, twenty-four poor and feeble folk were kept, at an annual cost approaching £49, while £69 was disbursed to feed those poor coming to the abbey for alms on an occasional basis. The closure of Whalley Abbey was a serious blow to many in the area. Not only was this poor relief withdrawn, but there were some ninety paid servants who would have encountered great difficulty in finding new employment, with many having themselves to rely on charity.

The ruins of Whalley Abbey are well known. As with many monasteries a private house, occupied by various families over the centuries, was built alongside the slighted remains of the church and cloister range. The site was acquired by the Anglican diocese of Manchester in 1923. In 1926 it passed to the new diocese of Blackburn under which it has again become a centre for religious learning, and quite contemplation.

HORNBY PRIORY,
DEDICATED TO ST. WILFRED

Hornby Priory was a small and somewhat obscure religious house in the Lune Valley. Its foundation marks the beginning of a long connection between north Lancashire and the Premonstratensian abbey of Croxton in Leicestershire, and represents yet another example of long-distance contact and communication between a landholder in one part of the country and a religious house in another. The date of its foundation is uncertain, as is the identity of its founder. Croxton Abbey had been founded c.1159 by William, earl of Warenne and count of Boulogne and Mortain who, among his many landholdings and titles, was lord of the honour of Lancaster. This established the link with a Leicestershire house and it was not long before the principal Lune Valley landholders, the Montbegon family, had founded a small Premonstratensian house on their own estate at Hornby with direct links to the much larger house set up by their feudal superior. The actual foundation date has been thought to be c.1172 which would indicate Roger de Montbegon III as its founder. If, however, the foundation date is earlier, the founder could have been Roger's father, Adam, or even his grandfather, Roger II. The only recorded land-donor of any significance is Roger III who gave, in '*frankalmoign*', to the canons of Hornby, 100 acres of land in his township of Hornby.

There were other land transactions but these were of such minor character as to add very little to the house's wealth or status. For example, between 1220 and 1227, the master of Hornby, Richard of Croxton, received from the abbot of Cockersand, probably Hereward, and the canons of that house: a toft, four acres in one acre parcels at different locations, plus two and a half acres of meadow, together with common of pasture, easements and liberties associated with such land in the township of Wennington. There was a further gift, also in Wennington, of an acre of land and a perch of meadow, with associated common of pasture, easements and liberties, together with pannage of swine. The total area of these scattered parcels of land would barely amount to nine acres and would have represented to Hornby Priory little more than a few pence each year in rent from the villeins who cultivated them as part of Wennington's common-field system.

 Such a limited landholding would have ensured Hornby's status as a minor house indeed, had it been independent, but it was clearly a cell or dependency of the abbey of Croxton and it rarely had more than five canons in residence. None the less, there was occasionally a suggestion that Hornby was a little more than simply a cell, answered for by its mother-house. The general chapter of the Premonstratensian order was normally attended by heads of houses, be they abbot or prior. In 1476, however, when the general chapter was held at Lincoln we find the prior of Hornby, probably Thomas Kellet, attending in company with the abbot of Cockersand, probably Robert Egremont. Generally, however, the status of Hornby is clear. In 1292, for example, we find the abbot of Croxton entering into litigation on behalf of the hospital of Saint Wilfred of Hornby. In the case of a totally independent house, no matter how small and poor – Upholland Priory would be a good Lancashire example – the prior would have conducted his own legal affairs.

In 1535, when Hornby Priory's days were nearly at an end, the *Valor Ecclesiasticus* assessed its annual net income at £76, its gross income being £94 7s. 8½d. More than two thirds of this income was derived from two churches long associated with Hornby. These were the churches of Melling and Tunstall, both of which were appropriated to the priory, and from which, in 1535, the canons derived £66 6s. 8d. The income from temporalities amounted to £28 8s. 4½d. Regular outgoings amounted to annual fees of: £2 to the chief seneschal, Lord Monteagle (of Hornby castle), £1 6s. 8d., to Marmaduke Tunstall (of Thurland castle), seneschal of lands in Lancashire, 13s. 4d., to the (manorial) court steward, Thomas Croft, and £4 for alms to thirteen poor people from the estate of Roger de Montbegon.

Hornby Priory is one of the few religious houses to have surrendered twice to the crown. In 1536, the royal agents Legh and Layton, accused the prior, William Halliday, of immorality. Whether or not he was guilty is unclear. However, a charge of this nature need not surprise us since the pair levelled such accusations at many abbots, priors and religious up and down the country, the easier to bring about the downfall of the house. In 1536 the priory of Hornby was surrendered to the crown by Halliday and his two canons, Robert Derby and John Fletcher. This was quickly cancelled, however, and a new prior, John Consyll, was appointed. The final surrender was signed on 8 September 1338 by Consyll, together with canons John Fletcher and Thomas Edwinstowe.

The site of Hornby Priory was granted by the crown in 1544 to Thomas Stanley, second Lord Monteagle, and son of Sir Edward Stanley who had distinguished himself at the Battle of Flodden in 1513, and had acquired the Hornby estate, building the splendid tower of Hornby church as his own memorial.

There are no remains of Hornby Priory. It stood beside the River Wenning a little downstream from the bridge in the village.

COCKERSAND ABBEY,
DEDICATED TO SAINT MARY

About 1153 the manor of Cockerham, to the south of Lancaster, was given, by William of Lancaster I, *'baron of Kendale and lord of Wyresdale'*, to the large Augustinian abbey of Saint Mary of the Meadow, Leicester. The abbot and canons of Leicester installed a vicar to run the church and a steward to run the manor, seeing no necessity to send any of their canons, except on the occasional visit of inspection. The manor and church of Cockerham represented to the Leicester canons a very useful source of revenue. William died about 1170 and was succeeded by his son, William II, who outraged the Leicester canons by revoking his father's gift of the manor of Cockerham which he settled on his wife, Helloise. A little after 1180 he introduced to a site called Cockersand, within the manor of Cockerham at the mouth of the River Lune, *"an heremyt of great perfecc'on,"* by the name of Hugh Garth. Hugh set up, with the assistance of two men referred to as canons, a hospital for lepers and other sick people. The canons were evidently of the Premonstratensian order, and so, presumably was Hugh himself, since in June 1190 a letter from Pope Clement III refers to the *'Prior of the Hospital Monastery of Cockersand of the Premonstratensian Order.'* Before 1200 there is a reference to the *'Abbot of Cockersand,'* indicating a further consolidation of the position of this new and energetic community in its wild and exposed position on the edge of the sea. The place at which Hugh Garth established his hospital was evidently already one with an aura of sanctity. It was known as the site of Askel's cross, a name that suggests a religious connection, though we do not know who Askel might have been, or why a cross associated with him should have been placed in this bleak spot.

William of Lancaster II died about 1184, but his revocation of his father's gift of Cockerham to Leicester Abbey was maintained by his widow and her second husband, Hugh de Morville. This was too much for the abbot of Leicester, and while the Premonstratensians were building at Cockersand, he went to law to have them removed from the site, and the manor of Cockerham restored to the Leicester canons under the terms of the original grant by the first William of Lancaster.

The Chapter House at Cockersand Abbey; a thorn tree permanently bowed after years of exposure to the prevailing south-westerly wind
(Photograph by Hugh Sherdley)

It was evident that the Leicester canons had the better case, and the Premonstratensians at Cockersand would seem to have been of such a mind themselves, for they abandoned the site, their legal position evidently untenable. At this point, sometime around 1200, the most powerful man in North West England intervened on their behalf. We do not know if he tried to influence the legal proceedings but he did make material provision for the canons of Cockersand during the time it took for the law to determine the fate of their abbey. Theobald Walter, brother of Hubert, Archbishop of Canterbury, lord of Amounderness, High Butler of Ireland, and progenitor of the influential Butler family of

114

Lancashire and Ireland, undertook to maintain the canons until a settlement was made. A few of them went to the estate of Walter's friend, William de Burgh, at Tuam, County Galway, while the remainder went to Pilling, Cockerham's neighbouring manor. At Pilling they probably stayed in the parsonage of the ancient church, and while they were there, Theobald Walter gave to them, in frankalmoign, the whole of the manor, or '*hay*', of Pilling.

Significantly, Walter's gift was made, not when the canons were at Cockersand, but when they were at Pilling, and the wording of the charter makes no mention of Cockersand. A translation of the relevant extract reads:

> *I have given and granted and by this my charter*
> *confirmed all my hay of Pilling*
> *To God and the Blessed Mary and the abbot and canons*
> *of the Premonstratensian*
> *Order serving God in that very place, in pure and*
> *perpetual alms for*
> *the building of a house of the Premonstratensian order*

Virtually without exception, charters making gifts to religious houses name the house concerned, and this one does not. The only place mentioned is Pilling, which supports the view that the abbey was to be built there, rather than at Cockersand. The document refers to the canons serving God in that very place, and to building there a house of the order. It is extremely difficult then, to avoid the view that, at the time of his grant, Theobald Walter had Pilling in mind as the site of the abbey.

No such thing happened, although it is distinctly possible that building, on the site of the present Pilling Hall Farm, had commenced. At some point, probably in the early thirteenth-century, the legal matter was settled by a compromise, to the evident satisfaction of all parties. The manor of Cockerham was to be restored to Leicester Abbey, but the immediate site of the

115

proposed abbey at Cockersand was to be detached in perpetuity into the possession of the Premonstratensian canons. This site comprised 346 acres, which came to be regarded as a detached portion of the manor of Pilling.

The Premonstratensian canons at Cockersand had come, like those in the Lune Valley at Hornby before them, from Croxton Abbey, Leicestershire. Unlike Hornby, however, Cockersand was not a cell or satellite, but a fully independent abbey in its own right. The canons came back from Pilling and Ireland to their isolated outpost on the windswept shore. They came back for two principal reasons. Firstly, because the site offered them a remote and often unpleasant place to live their chosen life, the better to demonstrate their devotion to God. The second reason was much more practical. The site is on an outcrop of red sandstone, and so their chosen building material was immediately available, and free.

They built in the Early English architectural style, and had made much progress by the middle of the thirteenth-century. The chapter-house is thought to have been constructed c.1230. The abbey buildings followed the standard pattern of: church, cloister surrounded by a two-storey range containing dormitory, library, kitchen, refectory and all the other chambers we might expect to find in an English monastery of the period. Medieval monastery churches are frequently disproportionately large, some, such as Glastonbury, Saint Albans and Bury Saint Edmunds, being among the largest churches in the land. Cockersand church, though small in comparison to these giants, was, at 175 feet in length, far larger than could ever have been required for the liturgical requirements of some twenty to thirty canons. It was surmounted by a tower and a steeple. We have no physical evidence of this but documents of the sixteenth-century refer to a steeple with six bells. Such a steeple would have been a highly prominent landmark for many miles. A traveller on the road from Cockerham to Lancaster would have seen it plainly, far away to his left, while a mariner entering

116

the bay and steering for the Lune channel and the port of Lancaster can have had no finer mark on his starboard hand than Cockersand steeple.

Slender central column supporting the roof of Cockersand Abbey Chapter House; tiny human faces are concealed in the foliage on the frieze

Of particular interest at the site is the lack of fresh water. Most monasteries were built alongside a stream that was used for all domestic purposes. Failing the presence of a stream we sometimes find a well providing good water. There is no stream at Cockersand, and because of its proximity to the sea, a well would produce brackish water. There is, however, no shortage of rainwater which was channelled via guttering around the buildings, to a large cistern below ground at the west front of the church. This would have been a satisfactory arrangement, though flashings and guttering of lead would have had a deleterious effect on the long-term health of the inmates. Furthermore, the proximity of the buildings to the sea-wall meant that waves breaking at high-tide with a strong south-westerly wind would produce fountains of spray to be blown across the roofs of church

117

and cloister-range. Thus water running to the cistern was heavily tainted with salt.

The abbey acquired a considerable estate in its first few years. Theobald Walter started the process with his Pilling donation, which was followed by numerous other grants of land in various parts of Lancashire and beyond. There were holdings in Cumberland, Westmorland, Yorkshire and Cheshire, though none of these was of great size. In the Lancashire hundred of Salford the Cockersand canons acquired the manor of Westhoughton, (4,341 acres), in Leyland they were given the manors of Tarleton with Holmes (5,534 acres), and Hutton, (2,744 acres), while in Amounderness they received Little Singleton, where they built a grange, Medlar, and a substantial part of Preesall. There were also significant Amounderness holdings at Forton, Stalmine with Stainall, Carleton, Layton, Warton and Garstang. In addition, within all the other hundreds, there were numerous gifts of a few acres, made by people who had little to give, but were anxious to receive the benefits of the holy canons' prayers and intercession. In the hundred of West Derby there were donations of land to Cockersand in at least 70 manors. Many of these donations were too small to be run as part of the agricultural activities of the abbey itself. Only large holdings such as Pilling, Little Singleton and Hutton, were farmed as viable units. The innumerable small parcels, many of them simply strips, or even half strips, in common fields, were rented out to villagers. Surviving rentals show long lists of tenants paying a penny or two, and often a couple of chickens, for these small pieces of land. In all, Cockersand Abbey held some 35,000 acres of land, an estate that would, in another part of the country, have made it a wealthy house. This was not the

case in Lancashire, however, since much of the land was of poor quality, being either moss or moor. The vast Lancashire mosses produced only '*turf*' (peat) which was useful for fuel but nothing else.

We know a good deal about the men who came to Cockersand to serve as canons in that hallowed, but windswept, spot. In the abbey's early days, when surnames, nationally, were not common, we find simply Christian names such as abbots, Henry, Thomas and Roger. We can assume perhaps, that these early Cockersand men were part of the original contingent from Croxton, and that they were therefore not local. Once surnames had come into use, the commonest form in the north was the name of the town or village from which an individual, or an ancestor, had originated. This practice tells us that most of the canons at Cockersand were serving not very far from home. In the fourteenth-century we find William Preesall, John Eccleston and Richard Preston. At the end of the abbey's life in the sixteenth-century, twenty-one of the twenty-two canons who signed the surrender document had surnames that are places within twenty-five miles of the abbey.

Cockersand held two churches that were a valuable source of income to a house always struggling to meet its commitments. These were the parish churches of Garstang, and of Mitton, on the Yorkshire side of the River Ribble. It was common for monastic houses holding churches to nominate their own monks or canons to serve them as vicars. Cockersand followed this practice at both Garstang and Mitton, and also, because the two parishes were large, with a number of dependent chapels, a second canon was detached to each church to act as '*procurator*,' or administrator of the parish, and to supervise secular clergy engaged to provide services in the outlying chapels. Garstang was perceived as two townships: Church town and Market town. The parish church is now known as Saint Helen's, Churchtown, and one of its chapels, Holy Trinity, licensed in 1437, was in Market town. This chapel was to become the parish church of Garstang when Church town and Market town became two separate parishes.

In addition to canons detached to serve churches, it was common for houses such as Cockersand to provide priests to serve chantries. After the practice of endowing monasteries to pray for the souls of the living and the dead had come to an end - very few were built after 1300 - the setting up of chantries became increasingly common. A chantry was a chapel that could be a side chapel within an existing church, or a separate building constructed exclusively for the purpose of having prayers and masses said for an individual or a family. To provide these services the founder of the chantry would employ one or two priests who would have no other duties. Cockersand sent canons to serve at two chantries in the Lune Valley: one for the Tunstall family at Thurland Castle and the other at Middleton church. It was common therefore to find six Cockersand canons serving away from the house. There were also two chantries in Garstang church: one founded by the Rigmaiden family of Wyresdale, and one by the Brockholes family of Claughton-on-Brock.

 Life at Cockersand was often a struggle against the unrelenting elements and the limited resources of a religious house that was far poorer than its endowments might have suggested. For much of its life we know little of what went on, though from time to time we are given a glimpse of events on that lonely shore. For the most part, we must suppose, the canons conducted their lives with the utmost propriety according to the strictures enjoined by the founder of the Premonstratensian order, Saint Norbert, at the abbey of Prémontré in eastern France in the early years of the twelfth century. Occasionally, however, surviving documents record wrongdoings of one kind or another. In 1327, for example, canon

120

Robert Hilton was pardoned for the killing of canon Robert Preston, though we are not told the circumstances under which the killing occurred.

Most of what we know of events at Cockersand took place in the last fifty years of the abbey's life. This detail is contained in the reports of Bishop Richard Redman, the Premonstratensian Order's inspector, or *'visitor,'* as such officials were known. There are seven reports of his visits to Cockersand which tell us a great deal about the life and people who lived and worked there. Much of the detail is fairly bland, reporting that the abbey is well run and orderly, and even where complaints are made, they are mostly of a minor nature. For example, he says that the canons must wear the regulation dress. They must wear the proper footwear rather than slippers, and stop hanging coloured tassels down their backs. They must, he says, be satisfied with the food they are given, and refrain from grumbling about it. More serious matters are mentioned occasionally, as when Redman writes that canons must refrain from speaking ill of their brethren, and stop drawing knives on one another.

Inevitably there is some salacious detail. Young men, albeit in holy orders, and having taken vows of chastity, found themselves from time to time in situations that led to what Redman refers to as *'lapses of the flesh.'* In 1488 two of the canons, William Bentham and James Skipton appeared before the bishop to answer  charges of *'gross incontinence'*: Bentham with a woman called Merioryth Gardner, and Skipton with Elena Wilson. These girls were servants who worked in the kitchen, and such places within the abbey, and it is not difficult to imagine the development of a situation that led to a couple of young canons, who met them daily in the course of their work, finding themselves with feelings stronger than their vows. Redman conducted the hearing in the chapter-house, in the presence of the abbot and the entire company of canons. Bentham appeared first and admitted his guilt, whereupon the bishop ordered him to perform forty days of penance and to be exiled to Croxton Abbey in Leicestershire for three years. When Skipton appeared he denied the charge of illicit sexual activity with Elena Wilson, and called upon his assembled brethren to support his plea of innocence. Not one was prepared to do so, and Skipton received forty days of penance and seven years of exile, at Sulby Abbey in Northamptonshire. Like Bentham he received three years for immorality, and a further four years for denying it. Notwithstanding the severity of the punishment received by the guilty canons, they were back at Cockersand three years later, when Redman made his next visit. Fourteen years later, Skipton was elected abbot and spiritual father of Cockersand Abbey. Such an outcome may suggest a fairly casual attitude towards monastic vows, but in fact the Premonstratensian canons were simply following the precepts of Jesus on matters of forgiveness. They could do no other.

Temptations of the flesh also visited canons working away from the abbey; in all likelihood, much more so. In 1494 canon Thomas Poulton, who served the Tunstall family chantry at Thurland castle, was brought back to the abbey in disgrace for his involvement with two women: Margaret Ambrose and Alice Pilkington. Again, before the assembled canons in the chapter-house, he admitted his guilt, received forty days of penance and banishment for three years to the Lincolnshire abbey of Barlings.

When Henry VIII began to turn his attention to the monasteries as a source of revenue, Cockersand received a number of official visitors other than those sent by the Premonstratensian order. The first of these, around 1534-5, was John Leland, who evidently arrived on a fairly ordinary day since he described Cockersand Abbey as:
Standing veri blekely and object to all wynnddes

The next visitors were the royal commissioners whose task it was to carry out an inventory of goods and chattels and to place a value on everything that could be moved and sold. The group that visited Cockersand was made up of the men who visited Lytham Priory, namely, Sir Thomas Langton, Sir Henry Farington, Sir Thomas Southworth, Thomas Burgon, auditor, and Thomas Armer, receiver. Their inventory and valuation survives almost in its entirety, and it seems that nothing was ignored and nothing was sacred. They started with the altar-plate: the silver chalice and paten being valued at 49 shillings. There were various sets of priestly vestments, the most expensive of which being of green silk and valued at 40 shillings. Brass and iron candlesticks were valued at 2s. 8d.; the abbot's chair at 1s. 8d.; and 54 books of parchment in the choir at 66s. 8d. The six bells in the steeple, together with the sanctus bell, are listed at £60, while the lead on the roofs of church and other buildings is assessed at £66 13s. 4d. Most interesting perhaps, and certainly most controversial, are the 30 choir stalls, valued collectively at 66s. 8d.: exactly the same as the 54 books. These are the very choir stalls that are thought by some to be the magnificent examples now to be seen in Lancaster Priory Church. In 1535, according to the valuation made by these three Lancashire knights, an individual stall would have sold for a little over 2s. 2½d. It is hard to imagine the superb workmanship at Lancaster being worth so little, and others might conclude, therefore, that these are not the Cockersand choir-stalls.

The kitchen, the pantry, the brewhouse, the refectory, the library, all had their contents valued. Even the abbot's bedding was assessed; interestingly, at 13s. for a mattress and a few blankets and pillows, compared with 2s. 2½d. for an exquisite choir-stall. Having valued everything in the house, the commissioners moved on to assess crops and livestock. These, of course were at Pilling, the demesne, or home farm, of the abbey. There was little enough in the way of corn to be counted, since not much land at Pilling was under cultivation. In fact, at this date some 5,000 acres of Pilling's 6,060 was mainly moss, though some of it was salt-marsh. The greater part of the 1,000 acres in use was devoted to cattle, there being: 58 milk cows at 8s. apiece, 30 heifers at 6s. 8d., 42 stirks at 3s.4d., and 3 bulls at 7s. apiece. In addition to these domestic cattle there are listed 17 wild cattle and one calf at 6s. apiece. These are only the cattle belonging to the abbey, of course. There would have been plenty more cattle at Pilling, but the remainder belonged to the tenants and were not counted by the commissioners. This concentration on dairy cattle is a clear indication of the Lancashire economy.

The sum total of goods, chattels and movables listed in the great inventory is £366 4s. 1d.: a most impressive sum.

Listed by the commissioners are thirty-seven employees of the abbey, at Cockersand and Pilling. Edward Holme and Robert Croskell are described as '*hinds of husbandry,*' or farm workers, and were paid £1 6s. 8d. per year. Ten men, holding the senior posts, were each paid this sum. They included: the smith, the miller, two horse keepers, and the overseer at Pilling. Best paid of all the servants was a man called Plessington, whose Christian name has not survived. He was of a substantially higher social class, being described in the list as, 'gent.' His position was that of controller of

124

the household, for which he was paid the sum of £2 per year. Also included among the servants, but not named, are thirteen servants of the bakehouse, brewhouse, kitchen, pantry and buttery, who were paid between them the annual sum of £17 13s. 4d. It was this particular group of servants that included Merioryth Gardner and Elena Wilson with whom canons Bentham and Skipton went astray some fifty years earlier, and although Bishop Redman, in order to minimise the risk, left instructions as to exactly where women were to be allowed to work within the house, we might surmise liaisons in the generations of serving girls and canons that followed.

One final group of abbey residents is of interest, namely those who were living there in retirement. These include fifteen poor men who were given bed and board of the charity of the house. There were also ten poor who were fed daily from charity, but lived elsewhere. Five others lived in the abbey by foundation. These were 'corrodians' who lived there by arrangement with the abbot, having paid a sum in advance, the agreement being known as a 'corrody.' Robert and Marie Lounde of Skerton had made an agreement, probably with abbot Newsham, in 1529, that they might live at the abbey for life in consideration of £5 6s. 8d. per year. They were to have a house, together with all the fuel (presumably turf) that they required and a milk cow provided by the abbey. They were to receive eight loaves of white bread and eight of grey bread, six bottles of ale, with victuals and meat from

the kitchen daily, flesh and fish at noon and night as appropriate, all of which appears a good arrangement for the couple.

Despite the apparent value of its goods and livestock, the abbey was far from wealthy, and its annual income was such as to place it in the ranks of the poorer religious houses. Under the provisions of the Act of Suppression of 1536, any house with an

125

income below £200 per year was to be closed, its property forfeit to the crown, and its monks or canons offered the choice of: transfer to another house, a clerical post of some kind, or a pension. Cockersand, with a net income of £157 14s. 0½d., fell clearly within the group to be closed, but there was a last-minute reprieve. For reasons not altogether clear, though goodness of heart is a distinct possibility, the Lancashire knights who acted as commissioners raised the figure they were submitting as net income, to £282 7s. 7½d. This of course, lifted Cockersand out of the poorer class and ensured its survival for a little longer. The new lease of life was only brief, however. By another act of Parliament in 1539, all remaining houses were to be surrendered to the crown.

Cockersand Abbey surrendered without demur. Abbot Robert Poulton and his twenty-two canons signed the document on 29 January 1539, and at the stroke of a pen, the house that for more than 300 years had withstood famine, flood, tempest, scandal, marauding Scots and the Black Death, was gone. The abbot received an annual pension of £40, and twenty-one of the canons also accepted pensions, probably of £6. Only one canon, Abraham Clitheroe, elected not to take a pension. He was serving as priest of the chantry belonging to Sir Marmaduke Tunstall at Thurland Castle where he received a stipend of £6. No doubt he felt himself better off as a salaried member of the Tunstall household than as a pensioner fending for himself in the outside world.

The church and buildings were quickly demolished and carted away. The sandstone building blocks, already cut to size, were in demand and many may still be seen in the walls of farms and buildings in the area, indeed, a few elaborate window-heads have been incorporated in shippons at nearby Crook Farm. All that remains on the bleak and windswept shore is the chapter-house where business, both routine and extraordinary, was

126

conducted on a daily basis, and which became a mausoleum for the Dalton family of Thurnham Hall.

Doors in the Early English style c.1200 - 1300

MONASTIC MISCELLANY

THE FAILED MONASTERIES:

Tulketh Abbey, Dedicated to Saint Mary

Tulketh Abbey was founded in 1124 by Stephen of Blois, who was to become king of England eleven years later. It was destined to last for only three years, after which the founder removed his monks and resettled them in the Furness peninsula where they established Furness Abbey. There is nothing remarkable about a medieval religious community being moved to another location after such a short time. What is remarkable about Tulketh is that it was a house of the order of Savigny: the first house of that order to be founded in England.

The monastic order of Savigny was founded in 1112 by Vitalis of Mortain as one of the numerous new groupings of monks and canons coming into existence around that time. It did not last very long. In 1147 all the Savignac houses were absorbed into the Cistercian order and disappeared as a separate group. By this date there were thirteen Savignac houses in England and their absorption by the Cistercians was not at first something they welcomed. After a while they came to accept it but even then their more decorative architectural style marked out a number of their houses from those of their Cistercian brethren. The relaxing of some of the austere Cistercian architectural rules, such as happened at Rievaulx, can perhaps be attributed to Savignac influence from within the order.

Tulketh lies within Preston, in the western suburbs, though in the early twelfth-century the site of the abbey will have been in the countryside at some distance from the town. There are no remains and we do not know where the buildings, doubtless temporary wooden structures, were situated.

Wyresdale Abbey, Dedicated to Saint Mary

In 1196 the abbot of Furness sent out, at the behest of Theobald Walter, a group of monks to found an abbey in Wyresdale. Furness was by this date a large and wealthy Cistercian house that could readily find thirteen monks to go off and set up a daughter house. Likewise, Theobald Walter, the most powerful baron in the north-west of England, could allocate land and money to the setting up of monastic houses, as he did with Cockersand at this very time. The location of the short-lived Wyresdale Abbey is not known. It is generally supposed to have been at the place we now know as Abbeystead, a name which, according to place-name authority, Eilert Ekwall, means, '*the site of the abbey*'. It is not, however, called Abbeystead when it is first mentioned, some 120 years after the departure of the monks. In a document of 1324 the place we now know as Abbeystead is called, *vaccary del Abbey*. This name indicates a dairy farm or cattle pasture of the abbey. The '*stead*' element appears at a later date, and it is possible that the abbey was located elsewhere, with the *vaccary*, now known as Abbeystead, as one of its possessions along the river.

There is another use of the modern name. This is in Upper Rawcliffe where an area covering three fields beside the Wyre was known as '*Abbeystead*'. It may be that this was the site of the abbey, particularly since Theobald Walter appropriated the church of Saint Michael's-on-Wyre, just across the river, to his new foundation.

The life of Wyresdale Abbey was brief. By 1204, Theobald Walter had moved the whole community of monks from Wyresdale to his newly acquired estates in Ireland. He placed them initially in County Carlow in the south-east of Ireland, but this can only have been intended as a temporary expedient as within a year he had moved them to Abington in County Limerick which was to be their permanent home. It is doubtful that serious building work ever began on Wyresdale Abbey, and therefore there are no remains to be seen, even if we were sure of where to look for them.

Ornate window of the Early English period

THE FRIARIES

The two principal orders of friars, the Franciscans and the Dominicans, are called after their founders, Francis of Assisi and Dominic Guzman, who began their work independently of each other, at the beginning of the thirteenth-century. Both had in mind the salvation of the urban poor. Whereas the monks and canons built their houses chiefly in the countryside, the friars lived and worked in the towns and cities, among the very people whose souls they sought to save, and whose earthly troubles they worked to alleviate. The friars are also identified with scholarship. The growth of the various orders of friars coincides with the growth of the universities throughout Europe and much scholarly work in the thirteenth and fourteenth centuries, particularly in theology, was carried out by the friars. This is readily seen at Oxford and at Cambridge, where all the orders had large friaries housing a total of several hundred friars in each city, some belonging to the local houses but many from other houses who were there to study at the university. In consequence of this we frequently find doctors of divinity and other highly qualified theologians as heads of friaries, and indeed, as rank and file friars. At Lancaster, for example, where three priors are recorded, two of them were DD. These were John of Lancaster, who in 1410 was elected head of the English Dominican province, and Richard Beverley, who was prior in 1523.

The second important distinction between friars and monks, is that the friars held no property, either individually or corporately. Monks drew on the resources provided by their estates and churches; friars relied on the generosity of the people among whom they worked. They were known as '*mendicants*,' and their income depended on begging, small gifts, legacies, burial fees and the like. A monk was to be found singing the liturgy in his monastery; a friar's role was to preach the word of God to the poor and oppressed: in the streets and at crossroads, as well as in churches.

Friars came to England in 1221 when a Dominican house was established in Oxford, followed in 1224 by a Franciscan foundation in London. By 1350 there were some 200 friaries distributed throughout the country, with more than 5,000 friars at around that date. Other orders of friars established in England were: Augustinian or Austin friars (not to be confused with Augustinian canons) and Carmelites, together with a few houses of the minor orders such as *'Crutched'* friars and *'Sack'* friars – so called because of their coarse, shapeless habit they wore as an insignia.

The Dominican Friary of Lancaster, Dedicated to the Holy Trinity

A house of Dominican friars was established in Lancaster a little before 1260, by a local knight, Sir Hugh Harrington. Thirty friars are recorded in 1301, but these, as in other friaries were rarely there all together as many would be out on the road, preaching. In 1291 the house was required to provide three friars to preach the Crusade every year on Holy Cross Day (14 September): one at Lancaster, one at Kendal and another in

Lonsdale. At first, very little property was owned by the friary: perhaps a couple of acres and the site of the buildings in the vicinity of Sulyard Street. There were at least two extensions made and eventually the precinct covered twelve acres with entrances on South Road and Moor Lane. Much of this space was taken up by the cemetery, which lay between Sulyard Street and Moor Lane. The friars enjoyed great popularity in the area and many people chose the friary as their burial place, creating rivalry with the parish church.

Friaries, like the monastic houses, were subject to the Act of Suppression of 1536 and Lancaster Friary was surrendered to the crown, fairly certainly in 1539. In February of that year, Lancaster is referred to as one of twenty friaries still standing in the north which it was hoped would be suppressed before Easter, and on 10 March we hear of a royal commissioner, Richard, bishop of Dover, on his way to Lancaster, for that purpose. The site of the friary, together with those of the friaries at Preston and Warrington, was sold to Thomas Holcroft for a total of £126 10s. The property was later acquired by the Rigmaiden family of Wyresdale and then passed to the Daltons of Thurnham Hall.

There was a chantry in the friary chapel, founded by the ancestors of Sir Thomas Lawrence of Ashton near Lancaster. This will have caused some inconvenience to the commissioners as chantries were not suppressed until somewhat later. The chantry priest, Robert Makerell, was not one of the friars.

The Franciscan Friary of Preston, Dedication unknown

Preston Friary was founded around 1260 by Edmund, earl of Lancaster, although the site itself, lying to the west of Friargate, towards Pitt Street, was evidently donated by the Preston family. Building was under way in that year and in October Henry III, donated five oaks for building to the friars of Preston. There is some evidence of agricultural or industrial activity, in the form of a watermill, a windmill and rights of turbary. The friary has been described as *"small and square, with a chapel attached to quadrangular cloisters"*.

The original Franciscans, living in poverty, were known as the *'Friars Minor'*, but many allowed themselves to be drawn away from their founding ideals and there came about a different interpretation of poverty. They lived in a style similar to that of a monastery and came to be known as *'Conventuals'*. Some, however, adhered rigidly to the original principles of the order, and these were styled *'Observants'*. The Franciscan house at Preston was Conventual.

In 1291, the archbishop of York instructed that the friary should provide a friar to preach the crusade in Preston, and another at some populous place in the neighbourhood.

Very little recorded history has survived. Charges of dishonesty were brought against Thomas Todgill, the last warden of Preston Friary, but we know nothing of the outcome. The friary was suppressed in 1539 and the property sold to Thomas Holcroft.

The Augustinian Friary of Warrington, Dedication unknown

A little before 1308 a house of Austin friars was established at Warrington, probably by William FitzAlmeric Butler, descendant of the great twelfth-century baron, Theobald Walter. Other leading benefactors of the friary were the families of Tarboke, Atherton, Shireburne and Warburton. The site was situated near Pear Tree Croft where it seems that a former hospital

134

was taken over by the friars. Small, simple buildings were erected in the Early English architectural style.

The Austin Friars of Warrington were held in high public esteem. Their friary church was well attended and they administered the sacraments to large numbers of locals. To further this process, many of the friars sought ordination of the bishop of Lichfield, within whose diocese Warrington at that time lay. Young men joining the orders of friars were not ordained at that point, but, serving the public as they did, it was much more appropriate for them to be in priestly orders than, say, Cistercian monks who did not have much to do with ordinary folk.

The friary was surrendered to the crown, probably in 1539, and the property sold, along with that of the other Lancashire friaries, to Thomas Holcroft.

Little known Franciscan houses

The eighteenth-century English Franciscan, Anthony Parkinson, a Lancashire man, refers to a house of Franciscan friars in Warrington. The evidence he offers is not conclusive, and we cannot say with certainty that such a house actually existed, or if it did, then perhaps it was short-lived.

Parkinson also refers to a Franciscan house in Lancaster, and here we can be more certain that such a house did exist, though as in the case of Warrington, it may not have survived for very long. The site of the convent was evidently close to the river, a little upstream of St. George's Quay. Parkinson states that the site belonged in 1714 to the Daltons of Thurnham, and was let for £3 per year to Henry Westby, a miller. Parkinson refers to the enclosure wall of the convent that was still standing and sound in that year. In the case of the Lancaster Franciscan friary, and, indeed that of Warrington, we know nothing of a founder, a dedication or of any revenues. The suggestion that they did not exist for very long is probably the explanation for this lack of evidence.

Magnificent Early English door with wicket

LANCASHIRE HOLDINGS OF MONASTERIES
IN OTHER COUNTIES

Kirkham, property of Vale Royal Abbey

The manor and church of Kirkham was given in 1093 by Geoffrey, sheriff appointed by Roger of Poitou, to the great Benedictine abbey of Shrewsbury. Within a year, this gift had been rescinded by Roger himself, who gave Kirkham to his newly founded priory of Lancaster, but in 1140 it was restored to Shrewsbury. Title to the church and manor was obtained by Theobald Walter in 1196, and he agreed to pay for it by the sum of 12 marks per annum to the abbot of Shrewsbury. Kirkham passed through Theobald's family, which changed its name to Butler, and in 1279 the manor was held by Theobald Butler, great grandson of Theobald Walter. At this date it was acquired from the Butler family by King Edward I who had founded the Cistercian abbey of Vale Royal in Cheshire two years earlier. Butler disputed the claim to the manor made by the king and only relinquished title to it after protracted litigation. In recognition of Theobald Butler's agreement the king gave him a goshawk.

The king transferred the church and manor of Kirkham to Vale Royal Abbey, and it remained the property of the abbot and monks until the house was dissolved in 1538, after which it passed again to the crown.

Rossall Grange, property of Dieulacres Abbey

Shortly before his death in 1216 King John granted the property of Rossall to the Cistercian abbey of Dieulacres, Staffordshire. Though mentioned in Domesday, Rossall does not seem to have been regarded as a manor. It was evidently land that was unused and virtually unpopulated. The area is said to have been little more than a rabbit-warren, but it cannot have been this at the time of Domesday since the rabbit, or coney, had not yet been introduced to England. The Dieulacres monks were pleased with their new property and with the few parcels of land they received in the Fylde, at Great Eccleston, Freckleton and Thornton. They were also given, from each of seven manors, one *nativus* and his *sequela* (an unfree labourer and his offspring). These seven men, each presumably with a wife and children, were to provide a workforce for the setting up of a stock-rearing enterprise, and with their families, provide the nucleus of a new community. In 1270 Dieulacres received a further grant of land, namely 915 acres in Bispham and Norbreck which lay conveniently adjacent to their Rossall holding. Thus their total holding in Lancashire became 3,820 acres, almost all of it in a single block comprising Rossall, Bispham, Norbreck and a few acres in Thornton. The grant at Freckleton was one tenth of an acre, which seems likely to have been a building plot.

Rossall was so far from Dieulacres Abbey that a grange was established from the outset and the whole area given over to stock-rearing: mainly sheep, washed annually in Bispham Mere. An estate of this size produced a considerable volume of wool, customarily sold along with that of its mother house. Transporting the wool from Rossall to Staffordshire by pack-horse would have been a tedious, and dangerous undertaking. If, however, the little plot of land at Freckleton had been intended for the building of a store for wool, this would suggest an altogether different, and much more efficient mode of transportation. It is highly likely that Rossall wool was taken by sea, around the coast to Freckleton where it was stored before being loaded into river craft, taken across the Ribble and up the River Douglas, certainly as far as Wigan, as coal was transported in the opposite direction in later centuries. Even if the wool could be carried no further than Wigan by boat, the final part of the journey across Cheshire to the abbey by pack-horse would have been barely half the total distance

Rossall Grange, like other monastic estates was let to lay tenants from an early date. In the sixteenth-century, the abbot, William Allen, installed his kinsman, John Allen, at Rossall, and on John's death the tenancy passed to George, his son. George's

138

son, another John, was then granted a lease of the Rossall estate for his lifetime and the lifetime of his son, another George. The estate passed to the crown at the Dissolution but the tenancy agreement was honoured. Thomas Fleetwood purchased the estate from the crown in 1553, and he too continued to honour the agreement made between the late abbot and the Allens. John Allen died and the tenancy passed to his son, George, while Thomas Fleetwood died and the ownership passed to his son, Edmund. Eventually, in 1579, George Allen died, and only then did Edmund Fleetwood exercise his right to take possession of his Rossall property, according to the terms of the agreement made by Abbot William Allen some fifty years earlier. Amid much bitterness, George Allen's widow was evicted and Edmund moved in. It remained the home of a branch of the Fleetwood family for many generations, eventually becoming a noted public school. At about the same time, a little before 1840, the town of Fleetwood was founded on the estate, by Sir Peter Hesketh Fleetwood.

Accrington, property of Kirkstall Abbey

Towards the end of the twelfth-century Robert de Lacy gave to the abbot and convent of the Cistercian abbey of Kirkstall, Yorkshire, the whole of Accrington. This was a considerable acquisition for the monks and they set about turning it into an estate, or grange, in the Cistercian fashion. Houses of the order customarily held deserted land, which they used to good effect for both agriculture and stock-rearing. Where there were settled communities of villagers it was common for the Cistercians to evict them, which was precisely what they did at Accrington. The estate was set up and a grange built for the storage of produce and the accommodation of three lay-brothers to manage the abbey's affairs. The dispossessed villagers were incensed at what had taken place and they attacked the grange, burning it to the ground, destroying furniture and implements and, most heinous of all, murdering the three lay-bothers, Norman, Humphrey and Robert.

The outraged abbot called for justice to the patron of the house, Robert de Lacy, who rounded up the malefactors, together with their families and drove them into banishment. They were not to be restored to normal life until they had sworn to abjure, for themselves and their successors, any rights they might have in the vill of Accrington. They must also make financial recompense for the damage they had done.

Order having been restored, the abbot rebuilt the grange and brought the estate back into production. This, however, did not last for very long. In 1287 it was agreed that the estate of Accrington should be returned by the abbey to the de Lacy family along with lands in Cliviger and Huncote, in consideration of the payment of 50 marks a year in perpetuity. Interestingly, the abbot imposed a typically Cistercian condition on the holding of the land by the de Lacys, namely that it should be devoted to pious uses and perpetual alms.

The holding of Accrington by Kirkstall Abbey lasted for less than a hundred years in the thirteenth-century, and there is little now to show for it. Allusions to abbey, or grange in names about the town are no doubt related to this long ago period, though 'Black Abbey' seems an unlikely reference to Kirkstall since the Cistercians were known as the 'White Monks'.

THE KNIGHTS HOSPITALLER

The origin of the Knights Hospitaller lay in the Holy Land at the beginning of the twelfth-century. Like the Templars and other crusading orders, the Hospitallers combined the status of monk with the role of warrior, recruits coming only from the finest of European families, and committing themselves to a life of monastic austerity and military endeavour.

The order sought to provide protection and medical care for pilgrims to the sacred places, but its principal role lay in the military struggle against Islamic encroachment. To this end the knights received donations of land with which they financed their never-ending battle. The recruits brought with them their personal fortunes but the greater part of the order's income came from the lands they were given throughout Europe. Large numbers of donations of varying sizes brought into the Hospitallers' possession extensive lands, though often in small parcels rather than large estates. This was certainly the case in England, and the example of their Lancashire holdings is quite typical. The order built no great monasteries and was represented in England by a few retired knights, together with servants and chaplains. These individuals kept an eye on the estates, collected the revenues and sent off the money to fund the fighting men at the battle-front. It was Hospitaller policy to rent out their lands permanently to families, so that the tenancy was inherited by the next generation, at which point the incoming tenant paid a sum of money as a '*mortuary*' in addition to his rent. The order established a number of preceptories in various parts of the country from which to administer their lands, and within the area controlled by each were smaller establishments known as *camerae*, chambers, which gathered the revenue and paid it in to the preceptories.

In Lancashire there were two *camerae*: Much Woolton, near Liverpool, responsible for rents south of the Ribble, payable to the preceptory of Yeavely in Derbyshire, and Stydd, near Ribchester

141

which collected in the northern part of the county and paid the money to the preceptory of Newland in Yorkshire. It is impossible to know exactly how many individual holdings the Hospitallers had in Lancashire, but they were clearly numerous. Equally we do not know how much was collected for their war-funds year by year.

It will be of interest to list those vills and manors throughout the county in which the Hospitallers are known to have held parcels of land, whatever their size. Land is known to have been held in the following townships, although there were almost certainly holdings of which no record has survived: **West Derby Hundred**: Linacre la More, Haydock, Bickerstaffe, Down Holland, Abram, Halsall, Hindley, Parr, Sutton, Farnworth, Brettargh, Walton, Golborne, Hale, Kenyon, Flitcroft,Crompton, Shaw, Dalton, Woolton. **Leyland Hundred**: Bretherton, Wrightington, Longton, Croston, Clayton-le-Woods, Leyland, Becconsall, Whittle, Heapey, Parbold, Charnock Heath, Charnock Richard, Standish, Welsh Whittle, Shevington, Cuerden, Wyndle, Chorley, Euxton, Hoole. **Salford Hundred**: Wardley, Butterworth, Middleton, Buersill, Platt, Heaton, Ashton, Chadderton, Crompton, Wardle Anglezark, Blackrod, Aspull, Edgeworth, Swinton, Birtle, Milnhouse, Oswaldtwistle, Kenyon, Healey, Oldham. **Blackburn Hundred**: Dutton, Wheatley, Ribchester, Dilworth, Aighton, Chipping, Bailey, Accrington, Morton, Salesbury, Ediholes. **Amounderness Hundred**: Preston , Elston, Lea, Freckleton, Threlfall, Claughton, Bilsborough, Rawcliffe, Sowerby, Inskip, Thistleton, Cottam, Ashton, Comberhalgh, Ribbleton, Newton, Elswick, Eccleston, Warton, Goosnargh, Howath, Medlar, Stainall, Whittingham, Greenhalgh. **Lonsdale Hundred**: Lancaster, Yealand Conyers, Tatham, Kellett, Cartmel, Lindale, Ireby, Bardsea.

An example of the rents received is those collected at Stydd in 1535. According to the *Valor Ecclesiasticus* the order had £10 5s. 8d. from its lands north of the Ribble. Woolton is shown in

1338 to hold fifty acres of arable land and five acres of meadow together with a watermill, and collected £8 in rents. These estates were seized by the crown along with all other monastic lands and properties. In the main they were sold off to individuals such as Thomas Holcroft, of whom we have heard a great deal. The Knights Hospitallers continued their military struggle for several centuries, but were obliged to do so without support from England.

Cistercian monks at work in the scriptorium

GLOSSARY OF TERMS

ADVOWSON
   The right to present a clergyman to the living of a church
AID
   Occasional tax levied by a feudal superior
APPROPRIATION
   The alienation in perpetuity of a church to a religious body
BEADSMAN
   A layman kept by a monastery with no obligation but to pray
BRIDGE WORK
   An obligation to provide labour for the repair of bridges
CARTULARY/CHARTULARY
   A collection of documents such as deeds, grants etc.
CARUCATE
   From the Latin, *carruca*, plough: an area of arable land; perhaps 120 acres
CASTLE WORK
   Obligation to carry out maintenance work on the lord's castle defences
CONVENTUAL
   Following monastic routine in monastic buildings
CONVERSI
   The lay-brothers within a monastic community
CROFT
   A small, enclosed piece of land: perhaps two acres
DANEGELD
   A tax levied to bribe Vikings – continued later, after the Viking period
DEMESNE
   Manorial land not rented out but retained by the lord for personal use
DONA
   Occasional tax
FIEF
   An estate held of a superior under the feudal system
FORESTEL
   Rights of the forest: hunting, timber etc.
FRANKALMOIGN
   A form of feudal land tenure, held in return for prayers

GELD
   Payment or tax
GLEBE LAND
   Land set aside in a manor for the maintenance of church and clergy
GRANGE
   A barn for agricultural produce; also used to accommodate monks
   managing an estate at some distance from the monastery
HAMSOKEN
   The right to tether animals for grazing
HERIOT
   Payment in cash or kind to the lord of the manor when taking up a
   tenancy
HUNDRED
   Administrative sub-division of a shire; Lancashire has six: Lonsdale,
   Amounderness, Leyland, Blackburn, Salford, West Derby
INFANGENTHEF
   Authority to try and hang thieves within the lord's area of authority
   and OUTFANGENTHEF
   Authority to pursue criminals outside the lord's jurisdiction and
   return them for trial and execution
LASTAGE
   Toll payable by market traders
MANORIAL COURT
   Court held to conduct the business of the manor and to hear minor
   criminal cases
MARK
   Unit of account worth two thirds of a pound, i.e. 13s. 4d.
MESSUAGE
   Dwelling house with associated buildings and land: garden, orchard
   etc.
MOIETY
   One second part of a property or landholding, not necessarily half.
MORTUARY
   Payment to the parish priest of the second best beast of a man lately
   dead
MOSS
   Peat bog
OBLATION
   Gift or offering

ORATORY
A small chapel, especially for private worship
OISTRYNGER
Keeper of goshawks for use in hawking
PANNAGE
The right to pasture animals, usually pigs, in woodland
PONTAGE
Occasional tax levied for the repair of bridges
PRECENTOR
A minor canon in charge of music in a cathedral or church
PULTER
Man responsible for poultry
PYX
A small receptacle in which the Blessed Sacrament is reserved
QUADRAGENE
Forty days of penance and devotion
SCUTAGE
Shield money: paid in lieu of performing military service
SECULAR CLERGY
Priests who live in the general community and do not belong to an order
SEPULTURE
Interment, burial; a burial place
SAC and SOC
Feudal tenure of land involving payment of rent
SCOT
Occasional tax levied by the church
SIMONY
Improper sale of holy offices
SPIRITUALITIES
Tithes and other forms of ecclesiastical income of a church or monastery
TALLAGE
A tax on feudal dependants
TEMPORALITIES
The secular possessions and profits from them of a church or monastery

THEGNAGE
   A form of tenure, Anglo Saxon in origin, where a man held land
   directly of the king
TITHE
   One tenth of income or produce, paid annually to the church
TOFT
   A small enclosed piece of land, perhaps one acre
TOLL and TEAM
   Royal grant of a manor/ suit for recovery of stolen goods
TURBARY
   The right to dig turf (peat); the place where it is dug
VIEW OF FRANKPLEDGE
   A group of families, usually ten, with responsibility for ensuring the
   lawful conduct of each other. The arrangement was inspected, or
   viewed annually, by the sheriff or lord of the manor.
VILL
   A village or township
VILLEIN
   Unfree labourer on a manor or estate
WARREN
   The right to pursue small game: coneys, hares, partridge etc.
WASTE
   Part of a manor not brought into cultivation: woodland, scrub, bog etc.
WRECK OF THE SEA
   The right of the lord to items washed up on the shore within his
   manor

SUGGESTIONS FOR FURTHER READING

Atkinson Rev. J.C., *Coucher Book of Furness*, 3 Vols., Chetham Society

Farrer W., (ed.) *The Lancashire Pipe Rolls and Early Lancashire Charters*

Farrer W. (ed.) *The Chartulary of Cockersand Abbey*, 7 Vols., Chetham Society

Hulton W.A., *Coucher Book of Whalley*, 4 Vols., Chetham Society

McCann J. (ed.), *The Rule of Saint Benedict*

Roper W.O., *Cartulary of Lancaster Priory*, 3 Vols., Chetham Society

Webb A.N., *Cartulary of Burscough Priory*, Chetham Society

Baskerville G., *English Monks and the Suppression of the Monasteries*

Brown P., *Augustine of Hippo*

Colvin M., *The White Canons in England*

Crosby A., *Penwortham in the Past*

Dade-Robertson C., *Furness Abbey, Romance, Scholarship and Culture*

Dickinson J.C., *The Origins of the Augustinian Canons*

Dickinson J.C., *The Priory of Cartmel*

Ekwall E., *The Place-Names of Lancashire*

Farrer W. and Brownbill J. (eds.) *The Victoria History of Lancashire*

Fishwick H., *History of Poulton-le-Fylde*, Chetham Society

Gasquet F.A., *Henry VIII and the English Monasteries*, 2 Vols.

Haigh C., *The Last Days of the Lancashire Monasteries and the Pilgrimage of Grace*

Kapelle W.E, *The Norman Conquest of the North*

Knowles D. and Hadcock R.N., *Medieval Religious Houses of England and Wales*

Knowles D., *Bare, Ruined Choirs*

Lloyd T.H., *The English Wool Trade in the Middle Ages*

Marshall B.B., *Cockersand Abbey, Lancashire*

Marshall B.B., *Monastic Estates of Amounderness 1066-1540*, M.Phil. thesis, Lancaster 1999

Mason R.J., *The Income, Administration and Disposal of Monastic Lands in Lancashire*, MA Thesis, London 1962

Midmer R., *English Medieval Monasteries 1066-1540*
Parkinson A.C., *Antiquities of the English Franciscans*
Rosenthal J.T., *The Purchase of Paradise*
Southern R.W., *Western Society and the Church in the Middle Ages*
Youings J., *The Dissolution of the Monasteries*

Index

150

Subscribers

Edward Huddleston, Bentham
Raymond J. Pilkington, Blackburn
Michael Tyson, Claughton on Brock
Josie Potkin, Salford
Elaine A. Patrick, Farington
Michael Rogerson, Preston
Bill Shannon, Fulwood
John Wilson, Tatham
Raymond Faulkner, Halton
Roger B. Frost M.B.E., Briercliffe
David & Noelene Shore, Huddersfield
John & Kathryn Swindell, Burnley
Father Daniel Rees, Downside Abbey
Kenneth Porter, Huddersfield
Clive McLaughlin, Guiseley
Douglas Wilson, Todmorden
Dr. Jenny Woodcock, Aigburth
Philip Smith, Upholland
John Whitehead, Clitheroe
David Waddicor, Darwen
John Walker, Kirkbymoorside
Rosemary Leach, Crediton
Roy Howard, Aberdeen
Brian Farrimond, Ormskirk
June Kurtz, Penwortham
Mrs M. M. Gilbertson, Atherton
Tony Hilton, Wigan
Mrs Kim Griffiths, Wallasey
Valerie Wigmore, Crook o' Lune
Peter I. Vardy, Runcorn
R. Cizdyn, Lancaster
Mrs I. Cragg, Preston
E. Mike Atherton, Penwortham
Dr, Francis Dewhurst, Leicester
Jim Danby, Ashton on Ribble

Phil Calvert, Simonstone
Elaine Berry, Fulwood
Stephen France, Littledale
William & Jennifer Rainford, Pilling
Peter Dickinson, Amersham
James Rawcliffe Tomlinson, Ansdell
Thomas Rice, Orrell
Michael & Helen Piela, Preston
Alan Waterworth, Frodsham
Stuart & Gay Crook, Northwich
Vincent Gee, Walkden
Rev. Alan Postlethwaite, Lindal in Furness
G. McCormick S.F.O, Flint
St. Vincent's Parish, Over Hulton
Raymond B. Smith, Blackburn
Mrs Rose-Mary Foster, Wallasey
Warrington Library
Gordon Heald, Knott End
The Portico Library, Manchester
Mrs Rosemary Fitton, Rochdale
Brenda M. Fox, Garstang
Geoff Garnett, Newton in Bowland
John Collins, Feniscliffe, Blackburn
Canon Robert Bailey, Cartmel
Mr & Mrs F. A. Childs, Bamber Bridge
Canons regular of Premontre, Corpus Christi Canonry, Manchester
Fr. David Lannon, Salford Diocesan Archives
Peter Harrington, Ulverston
Peter Purland, Liverpool
Ms Linda Barton, Inskip
John Lynch, Whalley
Dennis Kellet, Thurnham
Paul Holden, Blackburn
Mrs June Cawthorn, Skegness
Dr Allan Miller, Wigan
Bevan & Barbara Ridehalgh, Stalmine
Eileen & Neville Webb, Formby

154

Mrs Julie Taylor, Bolton
Rev. Peter Cookson, Liverpool Metropolitan Cathedral
Mrs V. Anglin, Bristol
Alf Westwell, Crosby
Philip Hagerty, Worsley
Anne Mimnagh, Rainhill
Gerald J. Fogarty, Eccles
Hilda Eastwood, Poulton-le-Fylde
Jennifer S. Holt, Haslingden
Peter Garth, Galgate
James Drake, Preston
Tom Canty, Gateacre
Rev. Robert Livesey, Eccles
Mike Derbyshire, Quernmore
Peter Gigli, Poulton-le-Fylde
V. Rev. T. Dakin, Thornton-Cleveleys
Mrs Doreen Read, Heysham
Doug Seed, Fulwood
Ian Page, Liversedge
Chris & Heather Smith, Fleetwood
Philip Sargeant, Penwortham
John Dickinson, Halton
Julia McLaughlin Cook, Liverpool
Bill Worthington, Penwortham
Bill Hosfield, Halton
Michael Lawson, Chadderton
Stuart & Gillian Jamieson, Eccleston, Chorley
Graham Keevill, Didcot
Alan Webster, Hornby
Chris Dawson, Great Crosby
Richard Anselm Austin, Gt. Harwood
William & Marian Bishop-Miller, Kirkby in Furness
N. O. Livsey, Salterforth
Ronald George Higginbottom, Timperley
Ian Glover, Halton-on-Lune
Paul Bannister, Blackburn
James Rothwell, Blackley

Alan D. Airth, Ellel
Alan F. Ashton, M.B.E., Lytham
Bruce & Marian Kitchin, Blackburn
David S. Johnson, Settle